Best Ever Craft Book for Kids

This is a Parragon Publishing book
This edition published in 2006

Parragon
Queen Street House
4 Queen Street
Bath BA1 1HE, UK

ISBN 1-40546-496-8
Printed in China

Best Ever Craft Book for Kids

p

Contents

MODELING

TOYS and GAMES

SPECIAL OCCASIONS

NATURECRAFT

Measurements and recipes

Follow these recipes for perfect papier-mâché and super salt dough. Use them for the projects in this book or create your own masterpieces!

Papier-mâché

Papier-mâché is perfect for making all kinds of models. There are lots of different recipes, but this is the easiest.

You will need:

✦ Newspaper, torn into short strips.
✦ Dish of white glue, mixed with an equal amount of water (you can add a little wallpaper paste if you like).
✦ Old paintbrush.

Paint the strips of paper with glue on both sides, using a paintbrush. Place the strips one at a time over the object to be covered and smooth them down with your hands. Add one layer at a time. Don't put too many on at once or it will take too long to dry.

You can make a bowl either by covering a balloon (p.128) or wrapping layers around a real bowl. If you do this, smear petroleum jelly over the bowl before you start so the model will slip off easily when it's dry.

Salt dough

This recipe will make enough salt dough for the basket on p.140. You'll only need one quarter of the recipe to make sherriff's badges (p.142).

You will need:

- ¾ cup all purpose flour
- 3 tbsp salt
- 1 teaspoon cooking oil
- ⅓ cup water
- Mixing bowl
- Board

Mix together the flour, salt, and cooking oil in a bowl using your fingers. Add a little water and mix it in thoroughly until you have a smooth and thick dough dry enough not to stick to the sides of the bowl. If your mixture is too sticky, simply add more flour. If it's too crumbly, add water.

Sprinkle a little flour over the board and knead the dough on it until it is a smooth lump. You can store the dough in a sealed container in the fridge for a couple of days.

Bake in a preheated oven at 250°F for about three hours until firm. Baking times will vary depending on the size and thickness of your object, but make sure it's hard all through.

Baking Tips

To get the best results, always measure your ingredients carefully. Ask an adult to help you when using sharp knives or scissors, or a hot oven. Always wear oven mitts when removing anything from a hot oven.

Get crafty!

Here's the inside facts on the best materials to use, and ways to save your hard-earned pocket money by becoming a crafty collector.

Essentials

It's a good idea to keep all your craft materials together. You could design your own craft box from the project on p.62.

Here's a useful list of the things you'll need to do most of the projects in this book. And don't forget—birthdays and Christmas are useful times to ask for that special set of paints you can't afford to buy yourself.

✦ A set of acrylic or poster paints and brushes
✦ Colored pencils and felt-tipped pens
✦ A pot of white glue and an old brush
✦ Scissors—the ones with rounded ends are the safest.
✦ Black fine-tipped fiber pen
✦ Pencil, ruler, and an eraser for those little mistakes.

Materials

There are some things you have to buy, but you can recycle or go hunting for lots of stuff. See how good you can get at finding craft materials for free. It's really fun!

Saving paper

No more ripping wrapping off presents. A crafty collector saves wrapping paper. If it's very crumpled, get an adult to iron it with a cool iron, and it will be as good as new.

Cardboard

Cardboard comes in different thicknesses. Often, you can use recycled cardboard instead of buying it, so save all your cereal and laundry detergent boxes. Large objects are often delivered in cardboard boxes, so keep an eye out for it.

Fabric

Have you grown out of your favorite jeans? Don't worry! You can recycle them. Denim can be turned into bags, purses, pencil cases—the list is endless! Save scraps of patterned fabric too. They can be used to decorate your creations.

Odds and ends

The crafty collector knows that buttons and beads make great decorations. You can make monster eyes from buttons and jewelry from beads. Even bottle tops come in handy!

Nature trail

When you're outside, you'll come across all kinds of things to add to your collection. Pick up leaves, twigs, feathers, and seed heads in the park and collect flowers from the garden to dry, but ask first before you pick any prize blooms! At the beach, look for interesting pebbles and shells for your collection.

Tips for success

Follow these simple rules and all your projects will be a rip-roaring success.

1. Protect from mess

If you're working on something messy, make sure you cover your workspace with newspaper or a paper tablecloth first. And wear clothes you don't mind getting spattered. Save your new running shoes for another day!

2. Wash your hands

Make sure your hands are really clean before you start. Nothing looks worse that a lovely handmade card with a big, grubby thumbprint right in the middle of it!

3. Be patient

Sometimes you have to leave paint, glue or clay to dry. No matter how eager you are to get on with your creation, it's worth waiting because your results will be so much better.

4. Use your ruler

If a project gives you measurements, make sure you measure as accurately as you can. Success might depend on it!

5. Follow the steps

Try to follow each step carefully. We've tested all the projects, and we know they work. We want them to work for you too.

6. Tidy up

When you've finished, make sure you clean up any mess. Gather up all your materials and store them together, ready for the next time you want to get creative.

PAPERCRAFT

Paper poppies

These poppies look very realistic, especially when light shines through the crêpe-paper petals.

You Will Need

For each poppy:
- ✦ Crêpe paper in red, light green, and dark green
- ✦ Scissors
- ✦ 2 pieces green garden wire
- ✦ 20 small black beads
- ✦ Black felt
- ✦ White glue and brush
- ✦ Pinking shears

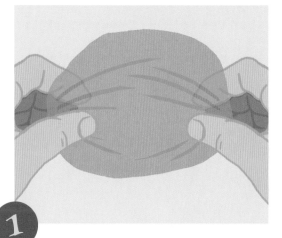

1 Cut out six circles from the red crêpe, about 3 inches diameter. Pull gently on each circle to stretch them into a dish shape.

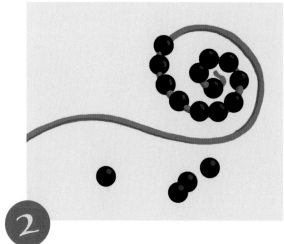

2 Twist the tip of the garden wire and thread 20 black beads onto it. Twist the beaded wire into a tight spiral shape.

3 ◀ Using the pinking shears, cut out a 2 inch circle from the black felt. Stack the paper disks loosely on top of one another with the felt circle on top. Poke the nonbeaded end of the wire through the center and pull it through.

4 ◀ Cut ¼ inch strips of dark green paper and paste them with white glue. Stick the top of the strip to the back of the flower and wind it all the way down the wire. Wrap a shorter piece of wire in the same way.

Try This!

Posy of pansies

Make these pansies in the same way, using lilac crêpe paper. Cut a figure-eight from the black felt and thread the wire with a single yellow bead to make the flowers' centers.

5 Twist the two pieces of wire together to make a stem and leaf. Using the pinking shears, cut a leaf shape from the light green crêpe and glue it to the underside of the leaf stem.

Cut-out supermodel

Do you see yourself as a fashion designer? Get creative and make a runway collection for your very own supermodel.

You Will Need

+ Fashion magazine
+ Tracing paper
+ Pencil
+ Colored pencils
+ Scissors
+ 11x8 inch sheet of thin white cardboard
+ Thick white paper
+ 2 toothpicks
+ Adhesive tape
+ Piece of self-hardening clay

1

Choose a photo of a model from a magazine. Trace the outline of her body.

2

Remove the tracing paper and transfer the outline onto thin white cardboard and, as shown above, cut it out.

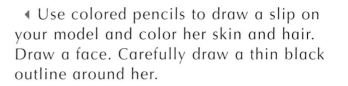

◄ Use colored pencils to draw a slip on your model and color her skin and hair. Draw a face. Carefully draw a thin black outline around her.

3

4

Put the model on a sheet of paper and draw lightly around her, so that you know the right size for her clothes. Make different outfits and matching accessories such as shoes and bags. Add tags to the clothes so that you will be able to attach them to your model.

5

Make a box-shaped stand out of self-hardening clay. Poke two holes in the clay with the toothpicks and leave to dry. Tape a toothpick to the back of each leg, leaving about 1/2 inch at the bottom. Insert the sticks into the holes on the stand.

15

Dinosaur mail holder

An armor-plated stegosaurus is just what you need to keep your important cards and letters from escaping!

You Will Need

+ 2 sheets stiff 11 x 8 inch purple cardboard
  + Tracing paper
    + Pencil
    + Scissors
  + Sheet of orange paper
    + White glue
  + 2 stick-on goggle eyes
  + Stick-on yellow spots
  + Black felt-tipped pen

1 Trace the templates on p.221 onto purple cardboard. Cut out two dinosaur shapes and two bases. Trace the face and neck onto one of the dinosaur shapes.

2 Trace the armor plates onto orange paper. Cut them out, making them a little smaller than your outline. Glue them, one at a time, along the spine of the dinosaur, leaving a border around each shape.

3 Glue on the goggle eyes and go over the face and mouth with a black felt-tipped pen.

4 Cover the body shapes with yellow stick-on dots.

5 Cut out four legs in each dinosaur shape. Cut two slots in the base shapes. Slot the shapes together so that you make a holder for your mail.

Mini gift box

This box is great for homemade candies, such as the peppermint patties on p.68. Wrap them in waxed paper and pop them in.

You Will Need

✦ Thick paper 16 x 12 inches
✦ Acrylic paints: blue, green
✦ Paintbrush
✦ Ruler
✦ Scissors
✦ White glue
✦ Small piece of ribbon
✦ Hole punch

1 Brush clean water over the paper. While the paper is damp, paint on blue and green stripes. The colors will run and make blurry stripes. Leave to dry.

2 Fold the paper in half and make a sharp crease. Unfold the paper again.

3 Fold the sides in so they meet in the middle, where you made the crease. Make sharp creases, then unfold the paper.

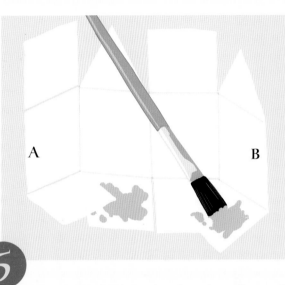

Only cut as far as the 4-inch folds you made!

A   B

4

Use the ruler to make two marks at 4 inches along each shorter side. Fold the paper at the marks, then unfold. You will have a grid of folds across the paper. Cut three slits along the top and three at the bottom.

5

Snip the 2nd and 4th tabs along the top into points. Now shape the whole sheet into a box by bringing the edges A and B together. Glue the bottom pieces together where they overlap.

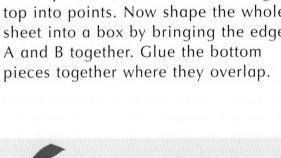

6

Use a hole punch to make a hole in each pointed tab. Thread ribbon through the holes and tie in a bow.

Piggy bookmark

Whether you name it Harry Hog or Tracy Squeaker, this piggy bookmark will help you keep your place!

You Will Need

✦ Strip of cardboard or thick paper 1 ½ x 8 inches
✦ Scrap of pink cardboard or thick paper 2 ¾ inches square
✦ Pencil
✦ Scissors
✦ White glue
✦ 2 stick-on goggle eyes
✦ Black felt-tipped pen

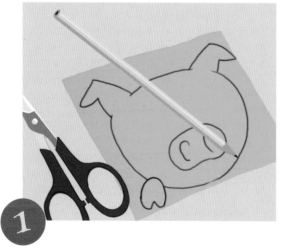

1 Draw the outline of a pig's face and two trotters on the pink cardboard. Cut out the pig shape.

2 Stick on the goggle eyes using the white glue.

3 Using the black pen, draw around the nose and mouth, then add nostrils and ear creases. Color the trotters black.

4 Glue the pig's face to the strip of card. Make the head stick up about 1 inch over the top of the strip. Leave it to dry.

Give your bookmarks a fluffy touch by gluing a few threads of wool to the faces.

Try This!

Animal Farm

Make a colorful collection of animal bookmarks for all your favorite books. It's a great way to use up leftover strips of cardboard from other projects. Try a pony, a cute cat, a dog, or even a penguin.

Ballerina card

This dancer really comes alive when you open the card and her tutu pops out!

You Will Need
+ White cardboard 8 inches square
+ Pencil
+ Set of colored pencils
+ Blue paper 12 x 6 inches
+ Scissors
+ White glue

Fold the card in half. Draw a ballet dancer, in a leotard and ballet slippers, in the middle of the card.

Color in the ballerina using the colored pencils.

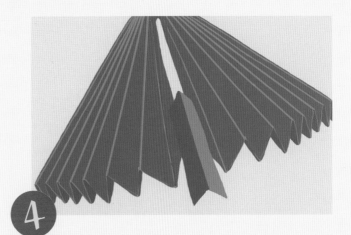

Fold the paper in half with the two shorter edges together. Cut a small piece of blue paper, fold it in half, and glue it where the two ends meet, making a fan shape.

Glue along the edge of the fan. Put the fold in the middle of the card at the dancer's waist and stick the two edges down. Fold the card closed. When you open it, a tutu will pop up!

Bubble-print gift wrap

Don't waste your pocket money buying wrapping paper. You can make bubbly wrapping paper instead. All you need is some dishwashing liquid, paints, and plenty of puff!

You Will Need

- ✦ Old newspapers
- ✦ Ready-mixed paints: red, blue
- ✦ Dishwashing liquid
- ✦ Water
- ✦ Old spoon
- ✦ Drinking straws
- ✦ Shallow bowl
- ✦ White paper

1 Cover the work surface with newspaper; this is a messy project! Using an old spoon, stir together ½ cup water, 1-2 tablespoons red paint, and ½ tablespoon dishwashing liquid in the bowl.

2 Put a straw in the paint mixture and gently blow to make bubbles. Keep blowing until the bubbles are almost over the edge of the dish.

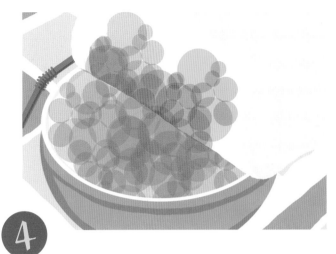

3 Put a piece of paper on top of the bubbles and hold it there until several bubbles have popped. Move the paper and continue popping bubbles until most of the paper has been printed.

4 Clean the bowl and make a blue paint mixture. Repeat steps 1 to 3 so you have a blue and red bubbly pattern. Leave the paper to dry.

Top Tip

If you don't get enough bubbles when you blow, add a drop more dishwashing liquid. If the bubbles are too faint on the paper, add more paint to the mixture.

Printed star card

Why not make your own stamps and try designing greeting cards? All you need is paint, funky foam, and some thick card.

You Will Need

+ Sheet of blue card 12 x 6 inches, folded in half
+ Tracing paper and pencil
+ 3 pieces funky foam 2 x 2 inches
+ 3 pieces thick cardboard 2 x 2 inches
+ Scissors
+ Poster paints: red, yellow, dark blue and brush
+ White glue
+ Red glitter

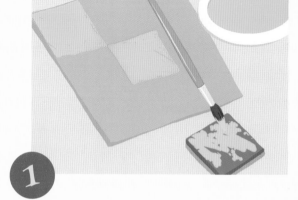

1 Stick a foam square onto a square of cardboard. Add yellow paint to your stamp and print it in one corner of the card. Print four more squares in the corners and middle of the card. Leave to dry.

2 Meanwhile, trace a star using the template on p.216. Transfer it onto the foam and cut out two stars. Stick each star to squares of thin cardboard.

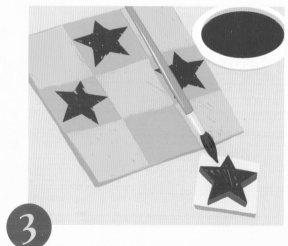

3 Add blue paint to one of the star stamps and print a star onto each blue square, pressing down firmly.

4 Use the other star stamp to print red stars on the yellow squares. Leave the card to dry.

5 Dilute a little white glue with water and brush it onto the middle, top left, and bottom right red stars. Sprinkle red glitter over the glued stars and shake off the excess glitter. Leave to dry.

Try This!

Gift tag

Make a matching gift tag by folding a piece of cardboard 4 x 2 inches in half and stamping each side. Finish by making a hole and threading through some red ribbon.

Groovy gift bag

If you have a gift that's an odd shape and difficult to wrap neatly, why not make this gift bag for it instead? It's really simple!

1

Brush glue on the white paper and stick the tissue paper to it. Then glue the wrapping paper to the other side of the white paper. Cut the glued sheets to 18 x 12 inches.

You Will Need

◆ 11 x 8 inch sheet orange tissue paper
◆ 1 sheet patterned gift wrapping paper
◆ 11 x 8 inch sheet of white paper
◆ Ruler and pencil
◆ White glue and brush
◆ ½ yard of red ribbon, ¾ inch wide
◆ 10 inches of pink ribbon, ½ inch wide

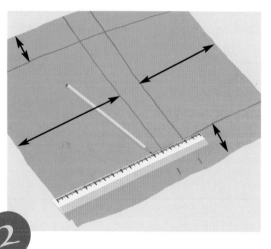

2

Draw two lines, 2 inches from the top and bottom of the sheet. Then draw two lines 8 inches in from the sides. Fold and unfold along the lines to make creases.

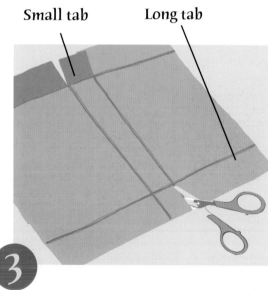

Small tab   Long tab

3

Use scissors to cut four slits up to where the lines cross, to make small and long tabs. Fold the two small tabs in.

4 ◀ This part is easier than it sounds! Paste glue along the four long tabs. Lift up the paper until edges A and B meet. Press the long tabs together then reach inside and pull up the small tags, gluing them to the sides. You will now have a box shape.

5 Push the sides of the box together and make creases, so it looks like a bag. Make three holes along each side of the top of the bag. Thread orange ribbon through the outside holes on each side for handles. Make sure you knot the ribbon on the inside.

6 Once you have put your gift in the bag, thread the pink ribbon through the middle holes and tie it in a bow.

Paper airplanes

These simple paper gliders have a clever secret to make them fly brilliantly. With a bit of practice, you can even make them loop through the air!

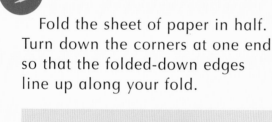

1 Fold the sheet of paper in half. Turn down the corners at one end so that the folded-down edges line up along your fold.

You Will Need

✦ Square sheet of colored paper 8 x 8 inches
✦ Stapler and staples
✦ Round stickers

2 To make the wings, fold the top down again, lining it up along the bottom of the shape. Repeat on the other side.

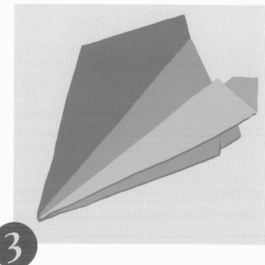

3 Fold the top flaps down again, lining them up along the bottom of the airplane.

4

Open out the folds that you made in the last step. To help the plane fly better, put two staples in the folded layers near the nose. Decorate the plane with round stickers on the wings and sides.

Floating glider

There are lots of variations of planes to try—this glider floats gently to earth like a seedpod from a tree. You can adjust the angles of the wings to make it loop in midair.

The triangular flaps at the wing bases will make the plane fly in different directions. Fold them up for an inside loop and down for an outside loop.

Top Tip

Your plane will fly much better if you fold really carefully. Line up each fold exactly before making the crease.

31

Cardplayers' wrapping paper

Give gifts a playing-card theme by stenciling the shapes of the four suits onto tissue wrapping paper.

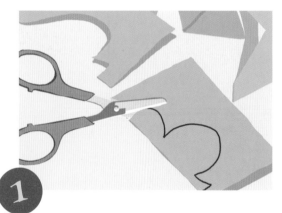

1 Fold each piece of card in half. Draw a half shape of a club, spade, heart, and diamond against the fold. Cut them out and put the shapes to one side.

◄ Put the gold paint in a saucer and lightly dab the sponge in it. Put the cardboard with the spade-shaped hole onto the paper and hold it down with one hand while you dab the sponge over the hole. Remove the card when the paint is dry.

2

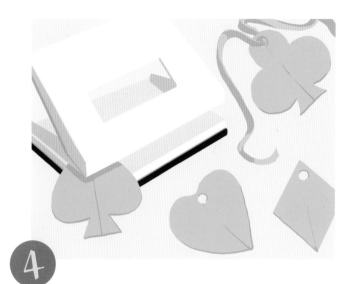

3 Repeat with the other shapes, leaving space between them so that you don't smudge your prints. Carry on printing shapes all over the paper.

4 Make gift tags out of the cut-out shapes you set aside in step 1. Simply punch a hole in them and thread a piece of thin ribbon through the hole.

Donkey peg

Make a useful carrot-crunching donkey clothespin to use on a clipboard or to decorate your bedroom.

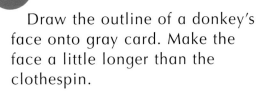

1 Draw the outline of a donkey's face onto gray card. Make the face a little longer than the clothespin.

You Will Need

+ Wooden clothespin
+ Cardboad: gray, black, white, orange, green
+ White glue
+ Scissors
+ Pencil

2 Now draw shapes onto colored cardboard: white circles for eyes, black pupils, eyebrows, mane, and nostrils, an orange carrot, and a green carrot leaves. Cut out all the shapes.

3 Glue all the features onto the donkey's face.

4

Paste a spot of glue on the back of the donkey, in the middle, and stick him to your clothespin. Leave it to dry.

Try This!

Cute cow

You can make all kinds of animal shapes to decorate clothespins. Try a cow made from black, white, and brown cardboard, and make a tasty daisy for her to munch.

Tissue-paper card

It's much more special to make greeting cards than buy them. Tear up some tissue paper and send a message to somebody you really like!

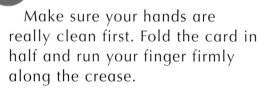

You Will Need

- ✦ 11 x 8 inch sheet of white cardboard
- ✦ Tissue paper: red, pink, blue
- ✦ White glue mixed with equal amount of water
- ✦ Pencil

1 Make sure your hands are really clean first. Fold the card in half and run your finger firmly along the crease.

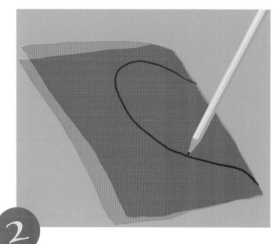

2 Fold the red tissue paper in half and lightly draw half a heart shape next to the fold.

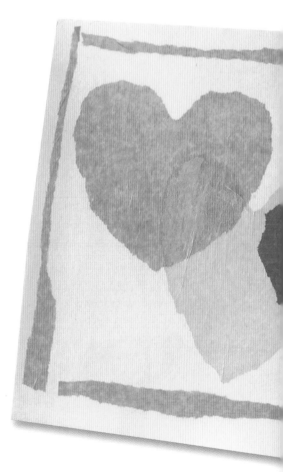

36

3 Slowly and gently tear the heart shape out of the tissue paper. Make different-sized hearts in the same way from the other sheets of tissue. Don't worry if they look imperfect—they're meant to!

Top Tip

If it's too tricky to put glue onto the hearts, brush a really thin layer of glue mixture over the whole card, stick the hearts down, then leave the card to dry.

4 Carefully brush the glue onto the hearts and stick them onto the card. Make the shapes overlap each other.

5 Roughly tear thin strips from the leftover tissue and stick them around the edges of the card to make a border.

Paper pompoms

Make your presents look really special with paper pompom decorations. Get some brightly colored tissue paper and you'll soon be going pompom crazy!

You Will Need

+ Tissue paper sheets in different shades
+ White glue and brush
+ Scissors

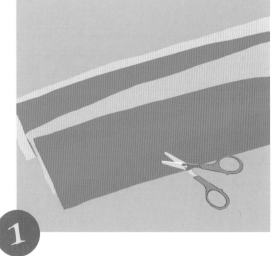

1 Cut two strips, 16 x 5 inches, from each sheet of tissue paper.

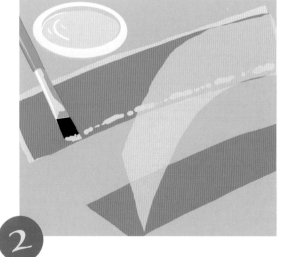

2 Brush glue along the bottom edge of each strip and stick all four strips together.

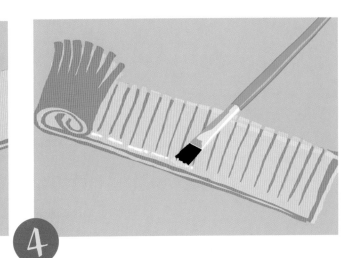

Make sure you don't cut from this glued edge!

3 Use scissors to snip along the strips, making each cut about ½ inch apart.

4 Spread glue along the bottom of the strip and roll the shape up. Press it together at the bottom and leave to dry.

Try This!

Foil pompom
For a special gift make a pompom using shimmery foil paper. Use pinking shears for a spiky look.

5 Use your fingers to fluff out the pompom. Dab some glue on the bottom and stick on top of a present.

Designer envelopes

If you enjoy making your own cards, why not design your own matching envelopes too? It's a great way to use up old wrapping paper.

You Will Need

✦ Sheet of colored 11 x 8 inch paper
✦ Patterned gift-wrapping
✦ Gluestick
✦ Homemade card

1 Put your homemade greeting card on the sheet of paper and fold the paper in on two sides and the bottom. Then fold over the top of the paper to make the flap.

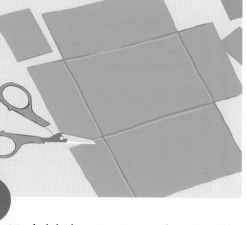

2 Unfold the paper and snip off the four small corner rectangles.

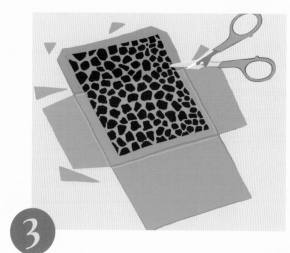

3 Cut a piece of patterned wrapping paper to fit in the top flap and main area. Glue it in place. Trim off the corners of the top and side flaps.

Be creative!
Make a colorful envelope from patterned paper and stick on an address label. You can easily make your own labels on a computer.

Maria

4

Fold up the bottom flap, then fold in the sides and glue them in place. Put in the card, then fold down and glue the top flap.

Top Tip
If your card is small, you'll get a neater effect if you trim the paper all around the card after finishing step 1.

David

Add colorful stickers to decorate your envelope.

Mosaic boat scene

Do you feel like a change from painting your favorite pictures? Stick colored scraps of paper onto your drawing instead, for a colorful mosaic effect.

1 Choose colored sections of old magazines. Tear out scraps of green and blue for the sea and sky, bright shades for the sails, and dark shades for the boats.

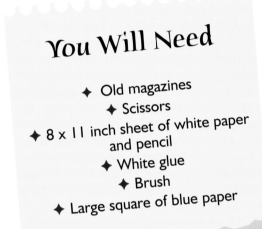

You Will Need

- ◆ Old magazines
- ◆ Scissors
- ◆ 8 x 11 inch sheet of white paper and pencil
- ◆ White glue
- ◆ Brush
- ◆ Large square of blue paper

2 Cut the scraps into squares of roughly the same size, about ½ inch.

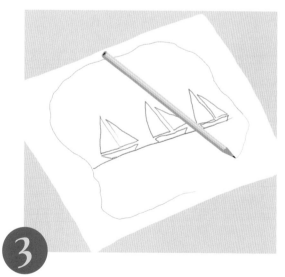

3 Lightly draw a seaside scene on the white paper. Draw a wavy line around the picture, as a guide to where to finish sticking squares.

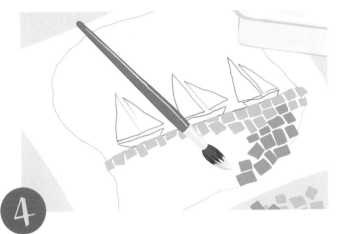

4 Start placing the squares onto your picture. When you are happy with the design, glue the squares down.

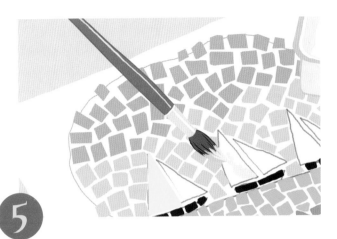

5 Make triangles to fit roughly into the sail shapes. Cut around the picture, then glue it to a larger square of blue paper.

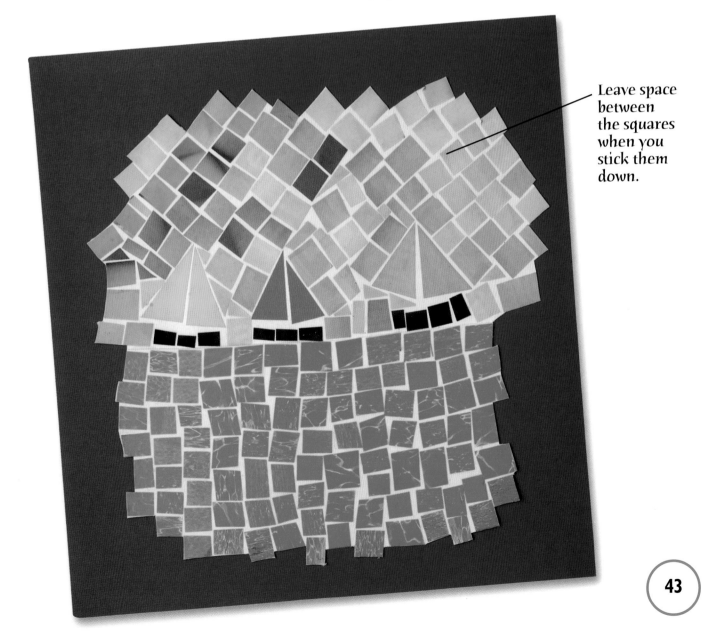

Leave space between the squares when you stick them down.

Wacky wastepaper basket

Brighten up a boring wastepaper basket covering it in wrapping paper.

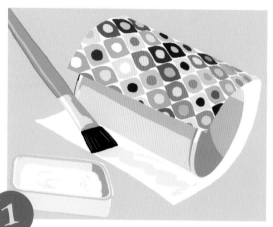

You Will Need

+ Round cardboard waste bin
+ Roll of gift wrap
+ Scissors
+ White glue diluted with an equal amount of water
+ Brush

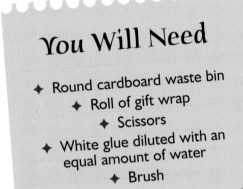

1 Cut a sheet of wrapping paper long enough to fit around the container, and 1 inch wider at both ends. Wrap the paper around the container and glue it in place.

2 Make small snips in the top and bottom edges, fold them over neatly and glue them down.

RECYCLE IT!

Bird feeder

Hang this handy feeder in your backyard and you'll soon have flocks of hungry birds dropping by for a snack!

You Will Need

- ✦ Empty, rinsed-out juice carton
- ✦ Sandpaper
- ✦ Scissors
- ✦ Acrylic paints: dark brown, light brown, black, white, dark green, light green
- ✦ Paintbrush
- ✦ Bag of bird seed
- ✦ Garden wire

1 Roughen the outside of the carton with sandpaper. Cut out a long window on the side opposite the nozzle.

2 Paint the carton brown all over. Leave it to dry.

3 Add long streaks of dark brown and white and small brown knots to look like bark.

4 Paint leaves over the carton in light green, with darker green veins.

5 Push a bag of seeds through the window and pull the top through the spout. Thread wire through the top of the bag and twist the ends together. Hang the feeder up outside.

Top Tip
Add a coat of varnish to help your feeder withstand the weather.

Yogurt carton herb garden

These cartons, planted with scrumptious herbs, will look great in the kitchen window. Don't forget to water them!

You Will Need

- ✦ 3 yogurt cartons
- ✦ Sandpaper
- ✦ Acrylic paints: red, green, yellow, white
- ✦ 3 jar lids
- ✦ Potted herbs: basil, oregano, chives
- ✦ Soil mix
- ✦ Awl or screwdriver

1 Wash and dry the cartons and rub all over the outsides with sandpaper. This will help the paint to stay on the pots.

2 Get an adult to help with this part. Make holes in the bottom of each pot with an awl or screwdriver.

③ Paint two coats on the outside of the pots: one each of yellow, green, and red. When the paint has dried, dab white dots on each pot.

④ Paint some jar lids to make matching saucers.

⑤ Carefully remove the herbs from their pots and replant them. Add extra soil mix to fill the pots. Press it down and water the herbs well.

Top Tip

Herbs taste great. Try adding fresh basil to tomato pasta sauce. Oregano is perfect for pizza, and minced chives are delicious sprinkled on top of creamy potato salad.

Blazing sneakers

Use fabric paint straight from the tube to make flaming streaks and a scary skull design on your slip-on sneakers. They'll help you run like the blazes!

You Will Need

- Pair of black slip-on sneakers
- Relief fabric paints: white, red, orange, and yellow

1

Use the white paint to draw a skull outline on the front of each shoe. Then fill in the skulls, leaving circles for the eye sockets and a double row of teeth.

2

With the red paint, draw flames on either side of the skulls. Fill in the bottom of the flames in red and leave to dry.

3

Use the orange paint to fill in the middle part of each flame and leave to dry.

4 Finish by filling in the last sections using the yellow paint. Leave the sneakers to dry.

Try This!

Party shoes

If you prefer a pretty princess look, stick on gems and use fabric relief pens to cover ballet slippers in a dotted flower pattern.

Top Tip
Sometimes the paint shrinks a little as it dries. Simply wait until the paint has dried completely then touch in some fresh paint.

Denim phone holder

Never throw your old jeans away. You can turn them into all kinds of useful stuff, such as this cool cellphone holder.

You Will Need

- ✦ Old piece of denim
- ✦ Pinking shears
- ✦ Red wool: Three 32 inch pieces
- ✦ Needle and red thread
- ✦ Button
- ✦ Fabric glue
- ✦ Scrap of red felt
- ✦ Scissors
- ✦ Craft knife

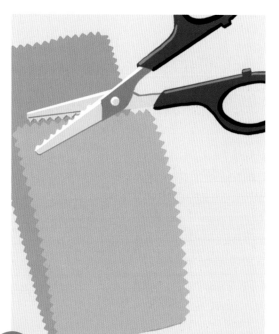

1 Cut the denim to 12 x 4 inches using pinking shears. Fold the fabric, leaving a flap at the top.

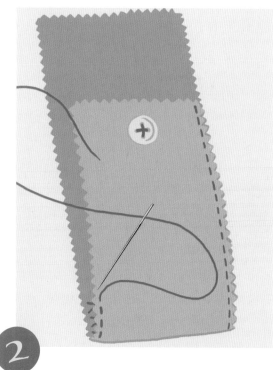

2 Use a needle and red thread to sew up each side of the holder. Sew a small button onto the front.

◄ Make a braided string. Put the three pieces of red wool together and tie a knot at one end. Braid the strands together and knot the other end. Stitch the braid to either side of the holder.

3

4

Cut out butterfly shapes from the red felt. Fold over the top flap and glue a butterfly over where you can feel the button underneath. Glue the other butterfly at the bottom of the bag.

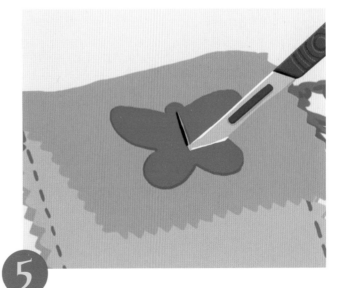

5

Ask an adult to cut a slit in the top butterfly to make a buttonhole.

Matchbox chest of drawers

You can store all sorts of things in this chest, from paper clips to buttons. And if you're a stamp collector, it's perfect for keeping your collection tidy.

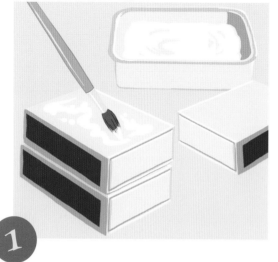

1 Glue three of the matchboxes together on top of one another. Do the same with the other three matchboxes.

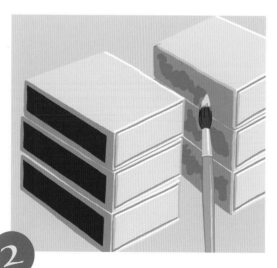

2 Glue the two sets of matchboxes together side by side. Leave to dry.

3 Remove the drawers. Use the end of a small pair of scissors to make a hole in the middle of each drawer. Push a paper fastener into each hole and bend the ends to fix them in place.

4 Paint the backs of the stamps with glue and stick them on the matchboxes. Overlap the stamps and stick them on at different angles.

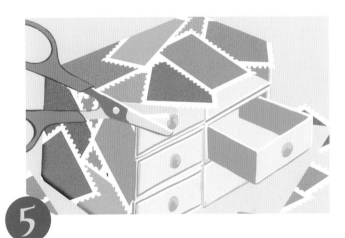

5 Trim the stamps where they overlap the edges of the box. Put the drawers back inside the boxes.

Try This!

Doll's house drawers

To make a doll's house chest of drawers, cut a piece of colored or wood-grained paper to fit around the box and the drawer fronts and stick on with the glue. Glue four beads to the base for legs.

Striped money box

Save your spare coins in a cool striped money bank made from a lidded cardboard container. You'll be rich before you know it!

You Will Need

✦ Empty cardboard container with lid
✦ Ruler and pencil
✦ 11 x 8 inch sheets of colored paper
✦ White glue and brush
✦ Craft knife or scalpel

1 Measure the height of the container and cut the paper to the same height. Draw lines down one of the sheets, changing the distance between the lines to make narrower and wider stripes.

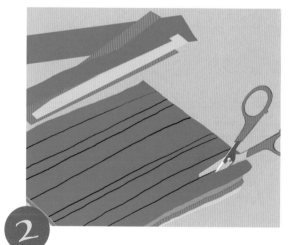

2 Put the ruled sheet with the lines drawn on it on top of the others and cut along the lines to make long strips.

3 Paste the strips with glue and stick them to the box, making sure they overlap and smoothing them down carefully.

4

When the glue has dried, ask an adult to cut a money slot measuring about 2 x 1/4 inches.

Try This!

Extra safe

If you're always raiding your money bank, make this no-lid version from a granola bar box. Use parcel tape to seal it, then decorate it with the paper strips. You'll have to break the whole box to get your hands on the cash!

Tiger feet

It's easy to turn old tissue boxes into striped tiger's feet complete with scary claws—they're grrrr-eat!

You Will Need

✦ 2 empty tissue boxes
✦ Acrylic paints: yellow, orange, black, white
✦ Paintbrush and old sponge
✦ Black funky foam and 10 double sided adhesive tabs
✦ Scissors
✦ Glue

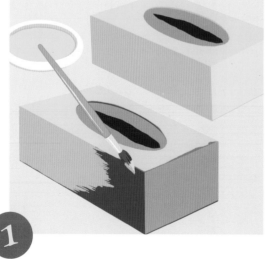

1 Using the yellow acrylic paint, paint the top and sides of the tissue boxes. Leave to dry. Apply another coat if the box color still shows through.

2 Dip a dry sponge in orange paint and dab it sparingly all over the boxes.

3

Paint black stripes about $^2/_3$ inch wide all over the boxes, tapering them at the ends. Don't worry if they aren't neat. This will make the stripes look more natural. Dab a few short white stripes on the edges of the black stripes.

4

Cut four pointed claws for each foot from the black foam. Make each one slightly smaller than the last. Stick them onto the box using adhesive tabs. Put the biggest claw on opposite sides of each box so you have a right and left foot.

Try This!

Zebra tissue holder

Make a zebra-striped tissue box by painting a full box of tissues white. After the white paint is dry, add black zebra stripes all over the box.

Racing yachts

These great little yachts are made from corks, and no matter what you do, they'll never sink. Try it and see!

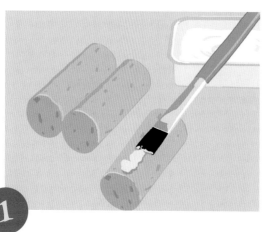

1 Glue the three corks together, side by side, using the strong glue. Leave to dry.

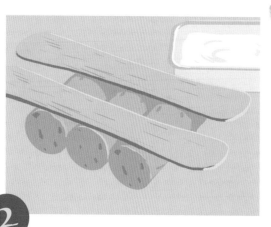

2 Glue the two popsicle sticks to the top of the corks as shown. Leave to dry.

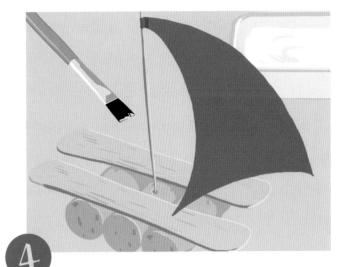

3 While the glue is drying, cut a triangular sail from one of the scraps of colored paper. Apply a little glue to the tip of the sail and wrap it around the top of the toothpick. Leave to dry.

4 Make a hole in the center of the middle cork between the sticks. Push the toothpick mast firmly into the hole. Bend the sail around so it sits on the top of the boat.

5 Cut a tiny triangle in yellow paper and glue to the top of the toothpick mast to make a flag.

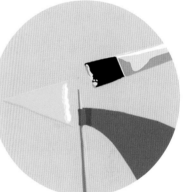

Try This!

One-cork yacht

If you don't have lots of corks, make a simpler version using just one. Push three map tacks in a row along the bottom of the cork to help your yacht stay upright.

Sporty storage box

This box will keep all your sports stuff together ready for your next game. Keep your room really tidy by making a matching toy box decorated with toy shapes!

You Will Need

✦ Large cardboard box with lid
✦ Large and small paintbrush
   ✦ Poster paints
      ✦ Pencil
      ✦ Paper
      ✦ Scissors
      ✦ White glue

1 Paint the box and the lid all over in green. Leave to dry, then paint another coat.

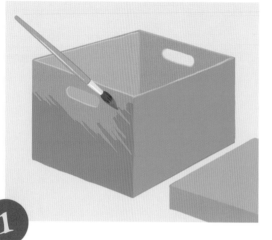

2 Draw the outlines of different sports balls and a tennis racket onto a sheet of white paper. Cut them out.

3 Use paints and a smaller brush to put the details on to the shapes.

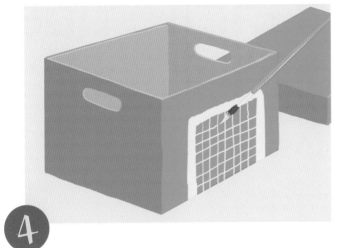

4 Paint a large white soccer net onto the front of the box.

5 Arrange all the sporting shapes around the box and glue them on. Leave it to dry, then get tidying!

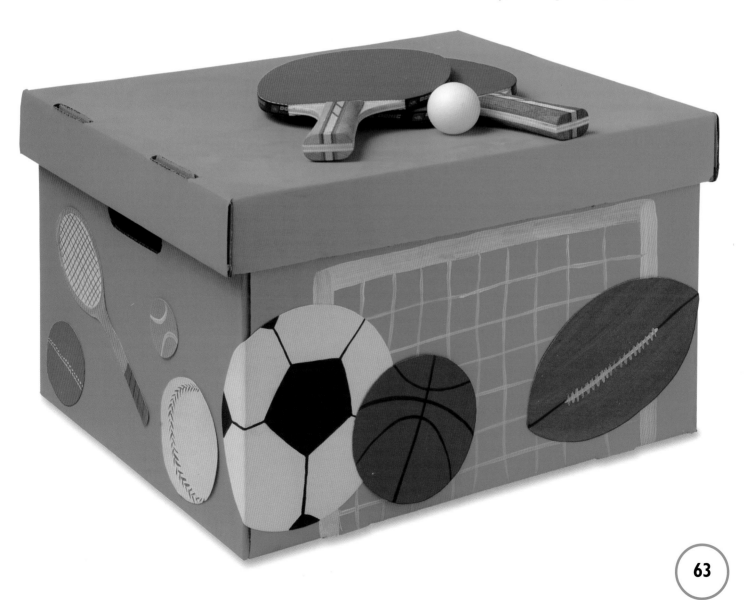

Starry pencil tube

Now you have a perfect excuse to eat a whole tube of potato chips. You can use the empty tube to make a cool pencil case!

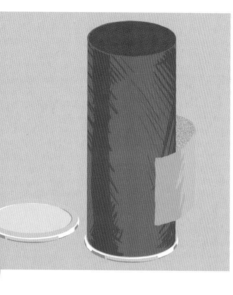

1 Rub the tube all over with sandpaper. This will help the paint stick better to the tube.

You Will Need

- ✦ Cardboard potato chip tube with lid
- ✦ Fine sandpaper
- ✦ Black acrylic paint
- ✦ Paintbrush
- ✦ White glue
- ✦ Glitter: gold, silver
- ✦ Scrap paper
- ✦ Sequins and star stickers

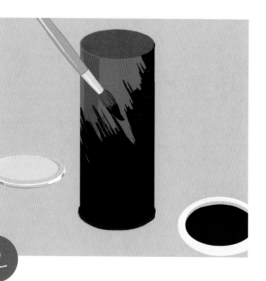

2 Cover the tube in black acrylic paint. Leave to dry, then give it another coat.

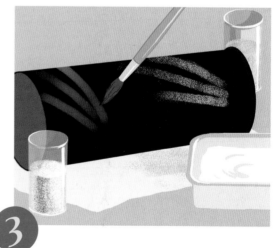

3 Make three swirls of glue like the tail of a comet. Sprinkle gold glitter over the glue and shake off the excess onto scrap paper. Repeat with silver glitter on other parts of the tube.

Try This!

Ribbon pattern

Make an abstract striped pattern on your pencil case. Paint the tube green then glue on long strips of colored paper in a random pattern.

Top Tip

Perfect for pasta

A potato chip tube is also an ideal shape for storing spaghetti. It would make a great gift for the chef in your family.

4 Stick on small groups of stars to make the heads of the comets. Stick other stars randomly on the tube. Glue a row of sequins around the top and bottom of the pencil case.

Popsiclestick pot

You Will Need

- Empty tube (i.e. a cookie tube)
- About 30 identical popsicle sticks
- Small set square
- White glue and brush

To make this pencil holder, you have to collect lots of popsicle sticks. Better get going!

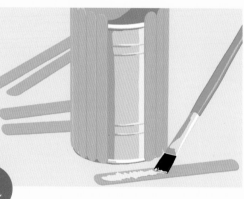

1 Wash the popsicle sticks and can in warm soapy water. Dry thoroughly. Apply glue to one side of one of the popsiclesticks. Line up the set square against the can and stick the glued popsicle stick in place, butting it up to the set square.

2 Glue the sticks around the can, until you have only 1-1½ inches of blank can showing.

◄ Paste glue onto three or four sticks and arrange them in the gap, spacing them out evenly to fill the space.

3

66

FOOD FUN

Peppermint patties

You'll need an adult's help to make these scrumptious sweets, but you won't need any help to eat them!

1 Sieve the confectioner's sugar into a large mixing bowl.

You Will Need

For 20 sweets:
- ✦ 4 cups confectioner's sugar
- ✦ 1 egg white
- ✦ Juice of half a lemon
- ✦ A few drops of peppermint extract and green food coloring
- ✦ Bar of baker's chocolate
- ✦ Sieve, bowl, cookie cutter, wooden spoon

2 Separate the egg yolk from the white—ask an adult to help you with this. Add the egg white to the confectioner's sugar.

3 Mix it all together with your hands until you have made a soft lump. Add the lemon juice, peppermint extract, and green food coloring.

68

4 Pour the lump out onto a cold surface and flatten it to about ½ inch thick. Cut out the shapes, put them on a tray, and leave them in a cool, dry place to set.

5 Break up the bar of chocolate and put in it a bowl. Put the bowl over a saucepan of simmering water and stir the chocolate until it has melted.

6 Take the bowl off the heat and quickly dip half of each sweet into the chocolate. Leave the sweets until the chocolate hardens.

Fruit smoothies

Ask an adult to help with the chopping, then whisk yourself a delicious, healthy fruit drink!

1 Chop three strawberries, the mango, and the banana. Put them in the bowl with all the other ingredients.

2 Blend everything until you have a smooth, runny mixture.

3 Pour the smoothie mixture into a glass. Cut the remaining strawberry in half and use it to decorate the glass. Add colorful straws.

Try This!

Frozen treats

Why not make delicious fruit smoothie frozen? Just pour the smoothie mixture into a tray, add a stick, and put it in the freezer!

This yummy smoothie was made with mango and pineapple.

If you prefer a sharper taste, go for fruits of the forest. You can buy frozen packages in the supermarket.

71

Pasta jewelry

Pasta comes in so many shapes and sizes that you can make a different necklace for every outfit!

1 Paint the pasta wheels in green, blue, and purple acrylic paint.

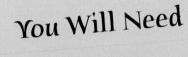

You Will Need

✦ Dried pasta shapes:
6 wheels, 24 curly macaroni

✦ Acrylic paints: green, blue, purple, gold

✦ Lump of plasticine

✦ Toothpicks

✦ Colored stiff elastic or cord

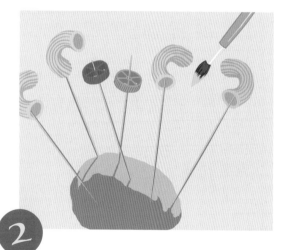

2 Paint the macaroni gold, and put all the shapes on the ends of toothpicks stuck in plasticine to dry.

Tie a button to the thread while you thread the shapes to stop them from falling off!

Try This!

Lots of choice

Your local supermarket has lots of different shapes of pasta, so go shopping for some inspiration!

3 Thread three macaronis then a wheel onto the colored thread. Repeat this until all the jewels are threaded.

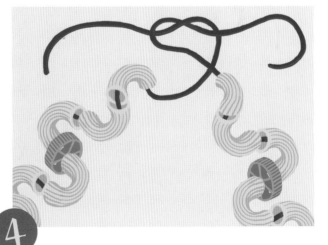

4 Knot the two ends of the thread together, making sure you have made your necklace big enough to go over your head.

73

Gingerbread Men

If you want to make this project even more quickly, get an icing pen from the supermarket. They're not expensive and are easy to use.

1 Heat the butter and sugar gently in a pan until the sugar dissolves and the butter melts.

You Will Need

- 2 tbsp butter
- 1/2 cup brown sugar
- 4 tbsp molasses
- 1 cup plus 2 tbsp all-purpose flour
- Pinch of salt
- 1/2 tbsp each baking powder, ginger, cinammon
- Gingerbread man cutter
- Rolling pin, cookie sheet, sieve, bowl, saucepan
- **Icing**: 1/2 cup confectioner's sugar, water, blue food coloring, waxed paper sandwich bag.

2 Sift all the other ingredients into a large bowl. Add the melted mixture and mix it all together until you have a soft ball of dough. Put it in the fridge for an hour.

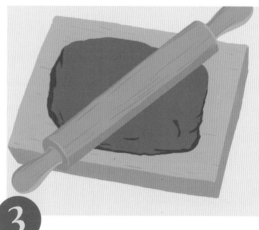

3 Roll the dough out to about 3/4 inch thick.

4 Use the cutter to make shapes in the dough. Put them on a greased cookie sheet and bake them at 375°F for five minutes.

5 While the cookies cool, make the icing. Sift confectioner's sugar into a bowl, add a few drops of blue food coloring and a little water, and mix until you have a thick paste.

6 When the cookies are cold, snip the corner off of a waxed paper sandwich bag and spoon the icing in. Decorate your gingerbread man by squeezing the bag gently so the icing comes out of the snipped corner.

Pirate treasure map

This battered map looks as if it has crossed the seven seas and been hidden down a pirate's pantaloons. But will it lead you to hidden treasure?

You Will Need

- ◆ Sheet of thick construction paper
- ◆ Bowl of warm water
- ◆ Instant coffee granules
- ◆ Paper towels
- ◆ Felt-tipped pens

1 Tear the edges from all around your sheet of paper to give it rough edges.

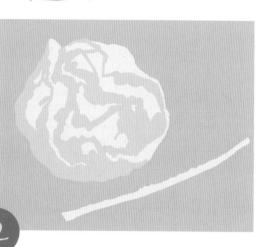

2 ◀ Crumple the sheet of paper up into a ball so that it is really creased.

◀ Flatten the paper and dip it into a bowl of warm water. Put the wet paper on the draining board and sprinkle over a spoonful of coffee granules. Leave for a few minutes.

3

76

4 Dab the stains with paper towels, then dip the paper in a bowl of warm water. Repeat the staining and rinsing on the other side of the paper. Leave it to dry out.

5 Draw a treasure map like the one shown. Add dangerous areas with a skull and crossbones and mark the hidden treasure with a big X.

Try This!

Skull seal
To keep your map a secret, roll it up and tie it with ribbon. Add a scary skull and crossbones seal made from modeling clay.

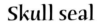

Fishy burgers

Everyone will love these delicious, healthy burgers. If you like vegetarian food, mash up a can of kidney beans and use them instead of the salmon.

You Will Need

To make 4 burgers:
- I small onion, chopped
- Pinch of mixed herbs
- A large handful of breadcrumbs
- 8 ounce can of red salmon
- I egg
- Salt and pepper
- A little flour
- Skillet and a little oil
- Lettuce, tomotoes, onion rings, mayonnaise
- Burger bun

1 Ask an adult to help with the cooking. Heat the oil in the skillet add the onion, herbs, and breadcrumbs and cook gently for 5 minutes.

2 ◀ Pour the mixture into a bowl and add the salmon, egg, and a little salt and pepper. Mix everything together with your hands.

3 Sprinkle some flour onto a work surface and shape the mixture into burger shapes, using clean hands.

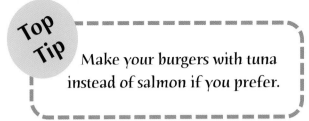

Top Tip

Make your burgers with tuna instead of salmon if you prefer.

4 Wash and dry the skillet, add a little more oil, and place over medium heat. Fry the burger for five minutes on each side.

5 Put each burger on a bun and garnish with lettuce, tomatoes, onion rings, and mayonnaise.

Choc chunk cookies

These star-shaped cookies are magic—they disappear in seconds! Mix in a handful of raisins or nuts instead of the chocolate for a tasty change.

1 Sieve the flour, salt, and baking powder into a large bowl.

You Will Need

- 2 1/4 cups all-purpose flour
- Pinch of salt
- 1 tsp baking powder
- 1 tbsp butter
- 2/3 cup light brown sugar
- 2 beaten eggs
- 2 ounces corn syrup
- 3 ounces semisweet chocolate
- Rolling pin
- Star-shaped cookie cutter

2 Rub in the butter with your hands, then add the sugar. Stir a beaten egg and the syrup together and add to the bowl.

3 Beat the mixture well with a wooden spoon. Add the other beaten egg. Break the chocolate into small chunks and add to the mixture.

80

4 Pour the mixture out and roll it to about ¹/₂ inch thick. Sprinkle some flour on it so it doesn't stick to the rolling pin. Use a star-shaped cookie cutter to cut out the shapes.

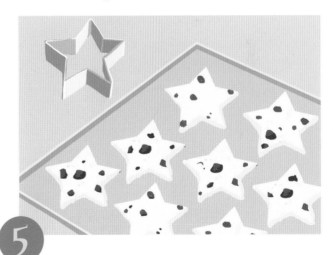

5 Put the shapes onto a greased cookie sheet that you've greased with a little butter. Place in a preheated oven at 325°F for 15 minutes, until they are golden. Leave them to cool, then enjoy!

Printed T-shirt

Do you think vegetables are yucky? Think again! They are perfect for making prints. Try this froggy T-shirt and see for yourself.

You Will Need

- ✦ T-shirt
- ✦ Piece of scrap cardboard
- ✦ Vegetables: 1 large and 1 small potato, 1 stalk of celery, 1 carrot
- ✦ Cutting board and knife
- ✦ Green fabric paint
- ✦ Shallow dish
- ✦ Tube of fabric relief paint: metallic blue

1 Ask an adult to help with this part. Cut the two potatoes in half and trim the top of the celery. Cut a 1¼ inch piece of carrot; then cut it in half lengthways.

2 Put a scrap of cardboard inside the shirt to stop the paint from seeping through. Pour some of the green paint into the dish. Dip a larger potato half into the paint, dab off any excess on the side of the plate, and make a print in the center of the T-shirt. This will be the body of the frog.

3 Use one of the small potato halves to print the two back legs. Dip the top end of the celery stalk into the paint and use to print a bulging eye. Repeat for the other eye.

4 Use the carrot to print the lower back legs and the front legs, then cut the carrot piece in half to print the front and back feet. Leave to dry.

5 Dab tiny spots all over the frog, using the tube of fabric paint. Leave the T-shirt to dry.

Try This!

Green gecko

Once you've got the hang of veggie printing, try different designs. This cute gecko was also made with potato, carrot, and celery, with yellow relief paint dotted over its body.

83

Cupcakes

Get an adult to help you bake these sparkly cupcakes. They're fun to make and even more fun to eat!

You Will Need

For 12 cakes:
✦ Heaping 1/3 cup sugar
✦ 1 beaten egg
✦ Vanilla extract
✦ 2/3 cup self-rising flour
✦ Silver foil bake cups
✦ Wooden spoon, dessert spoon, cookie sheet, and cooling rack

For the icing:
✦ 1/2 cup confectioner's sugar
✦ Few drops red food coloring
✦ Metallic cake decorations
✦ Butter knife

1 Mix the butter and sugar in a large bowl. Mix in the egg a little at a time. Add a few drops of vanilla extract.

2 Sieve the flour into the bowl and use a wooden spoon to mix it in gently to make a batter.

84

3 Place a spoonful of batter into each cup. Put them on a cookie sheet and bake in a preheated oven at 400°F for 10 minutes. Leave them to cool.

4 To make the icing, sieve the confectioner's sugar into the bowl. Add a few drops of food coloring and just enough water to make a paste.

5 Spread the icing onto the cakes. Sprinkle metallic balls on top and leave the cakes to set. Delicious!

Cress caterpillar

If you get tired of waiting for plants to grow, cress is the answer because it only takes a few days! It tastes great in salads and sandwiches, too.

1 Take five clean, empty egg shells with their tops lopped off. Trim the tops with nail scissors.

You Will Need

- ✦ 5 egg shells
- ✦ Nail scissors
- ✦ Paints: green, red, black
- ✦ Goggle eyes
- ✦ Paintbrush
- ✦ White glue
- ✦ Packet of cress seeds
- ✦ Cotton batting
- ✦ Red pipe cleaner

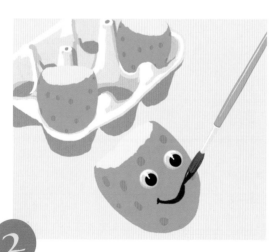

2 Paint the eggs green with red spots. Glue goggle eyes to one of them and paint a black mouth. Put them in an egg carton to dry.

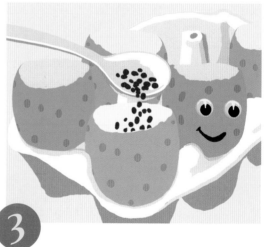

3 When they are dry, put a wad of cotton batting in the bottom of each egg, add 1tsp of cress seeds, then pour a spoonful of water over the cotton batting.

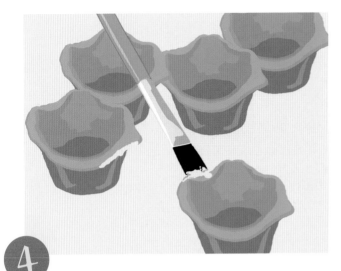

4 Cut up a cardboard egg carton to make five little dishes. Paint them green and glue them together in a wiggly line.

5 Put an egg in each dish, with the face at the front. To make antennas, twist a pipe cleaner into spirals at both ends, fold it in half, and push it into the shell with the face.

Top Tip Cress care
Don't let the cotton batting dry out. Add a little water every other day. The cress takes about a week to grow, then just snip it, wash it, and enjoy!

Chocolate banana sundae

Try this easy recipe or have a sundae competition with your friends. Invent weird and wonderful combinations and vote for your favorite!

You Will Need

- Vanilla ice cream
- 1 banana
- Chocolate sauce
- Cookie-decorating sprinkles
- Sundae glass and spoon

1 Spoon the ice cream into the bottom of a sundae dish.

88

◀ Add a layer of sliced banana and some chocolate sauce. Repeat the layers until you have only three slices of banana left.

This delicious sundae is made with peach ice cream, peach slices, and crushed meringue.

2

Fresh strawberries and raspberry ripple ice cream make a delicious fruity sundae

Top Tip Take the ice cream out of the freezer about 10 minutes before you start so it will be soft enough to use.

3

Decorate the top of the sundae with the banana slices, some more chocolate sauce, and the sprinkles

Clove pomanders

One of these clove-scented natural air fresheners in your room will soon get rid of that pongy aroma of old sneakers!

You Will Need

✦ Orange and lime
✦ ½ yard each of green and orange ribbon
✦ Toothpick
✦ Cloves

1 Put the orange in the middle of the green ribbon. Tie the ribbon in a knot then tie a tight bow over the knot. Repeat for the lime, using the orange ribbon.

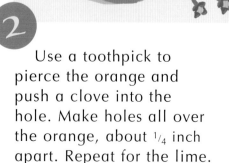

2 Use a toothpick to pierce the orange and push a clove into the hole. Make holes all over the orange, about ¼ inch apart. Repeat for the lime.

GREAT GIFTS

Fishy glitter globe

This is a great way to use glass paints. Design an ocean scene, fill a jar with glittery water, and shake up a storm!

1 If you want, arrange shells on the inside of the jar lid. Glue them to the lid and leave to dry.

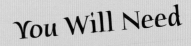

You Will Need

- Empty round jar and lid
- All-purpose waterproof glue
- Seashells (optional)
- Black relief outliner glass paint
- Glass paints: red, orange, green
- Paintbrush
- Glycerine
- Water
- Blue glitter

2 Turn the jar upside down and, with the black relief paint, draw the outline of fish and seaweed. Leave to dry.

3 Using the glass paints and brush, color in the seaweed and fish, blending the paints together. Leave to dry.

4 Fill the jar with water. Add a teaspoon of glitter and a few drops of glycerine.

5 Put a line of glue around the lid and screw it tightly to the top of the jar. Leave it to dry overnight.

Top Tip

Glycerine is great! It makes the water thicker, so when you shake the jar, the glitter falls to the bottom slowly. You can buy it in the baking department of your supermarket.

Shake the jar and place it upside down to give your fish a glittery sea to swim in.

Foil frame

Make a perfect picture frame from Tin foil and leftover cardboard. Nobody will ever guess you've been recycling!

You Will Need

+ Thick cardboard 5 x 5 inches
+ Thin card 6 x 6 inches
+ Ruler
+ Scissors
+ Tin foil 8 x 8 inches
+ White glue
+ Old pen
+ Small photo

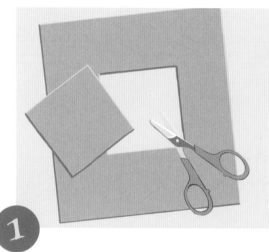

1 Cut out a 2 x 2 inches square hole in the middle of the thick cardboard.

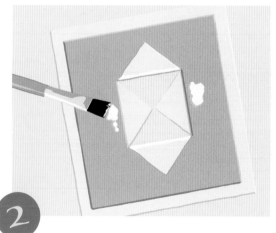

2 Glue the card to the non-shiny side of the foil. Make a hole in the foil and make cuts toward each corner. Fold the triangles you've made onto the back of the frame and glue them down.

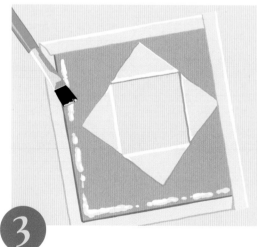

3 Now put a line of glue round the cardboard and glue the four foil edges to it.

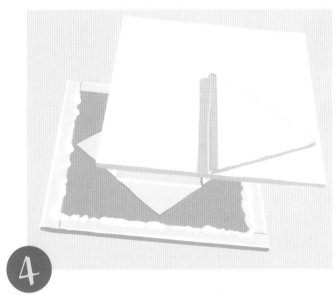

4 Cut out a triangle of cardboard and tape it to the square of thin card as shown, to make a stand. Then glue the two squares of card together around three sides, leaving a slot at the top.

5 Slide a photo into the slot in the frame. Using the empty pen mark your design on the frame. Don't press too hard or you may tear the foil.

Try This!

Heart frame
Cut out a heart-shaped frame and decorate it with heart shapes cut from foil candy wrappers.

Felt beads

This project is amazingly easy. Just roll up and glue colored squares of felt, then cut slices to make unusual spiral-patterned beads.

You Will Need

+ Felt squares, 3 x 3 inches: yellow, pink, and black
+ White glue
+ Scissors
+ 2 rubber bands
+ Needle and gold thread
+ 18 small black beads

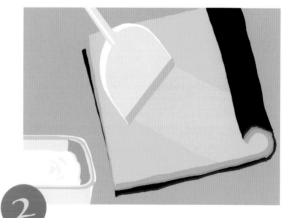

1 Spread glue thinly onto the black square and stick the pink square on top. Now spread glue onto the pink square and stick the yellow square to it.

2 Spread glue thinly onto the yellow square and roll up the layers to make a swiss-roll shape.

3 Hold the roll in place with a rubber band at each end and leave it to dry.

4 Remove the rubber bands and cut the roll into slices about ¹/₂ inch wide. Choose the best five beads for your necklace.

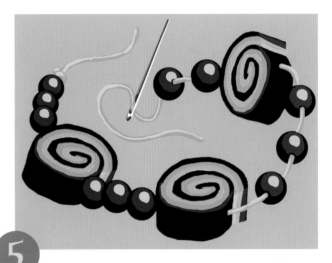

5 Tie a knot in the gold thread about 4 inches from the end. Thread on three black beads, then push the needle through the top of one of the felt beads near the join. Thread three more black beads, then the next felt bead. Carry on until you have used all the beads. Tie a knot in the thread and trim the end.

Try This!

Pink pendant

Make a pendant by gluing three felt beads together. Thread beads on as shown. Push the needle through the top of your trio of beads.

Candy cushions

These comfy candy-shaped cushions look good enough to eat. Make a pile and turn your bedroom into a candy store!

You Will Need

For each cushion:
- 1 piece of gold-colored fabric 20 x 28 inches
- 1 piece of colored netting 20 x 28 inches
- Newspaper
- White glue
- 2 strong rubber bands
- Cushion filling, such as polyester filing
- Half yard of gold ribbon

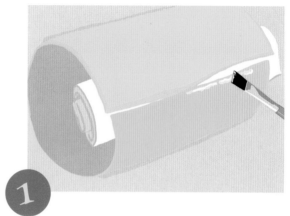

1 Glue the two pieces of fabric together along the longer edges. Stick the short edges together to make a tube. Put newspaper inside to stop the glued seam from sticking to the other side. Leave it to dry.

2 Gather up one end about 5 inches from the edge and hold it in place with one of the rubber bands. Wind the band around several times to make it secure.

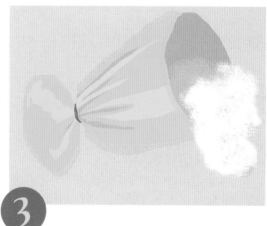

3 Start stuffing the cushion with the filling until it has filled to about 5 inches from the top.

4 Close the end with the other rubber band. Fan out the ends of the cushion to make them look like candy wrappers.

5 Glue some gold ribbon over the rubber bands so they don't show.

Top Tip Recycle old cushions by unpicking the seams and reusing the filling for your groovy new cushions.

Silhouette hanging

This moonlit woodland scene is made from acetate and cardboard, but it looks just like stained glass!

You Will Need

- ✦ Pair of compasses
- ✦ 3 8 x 11 inch sheets of black cardboard
- ✦ Blue acetate film
- ✦ Scissors
- ✦ Pencil
- ✦ White glue and brush
- ✦ Hole punch

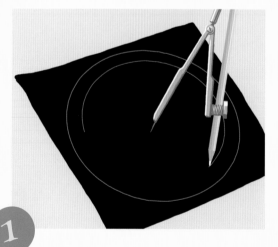

1 Use the compasses to make an 8-inch circle on the black card. Draw another circle ³/₄ inch in from the first.

2 Cut out the ring shape, draw around it onto the other piece of card and cut that one out too. Now you have two black rings.

On another piece of black cardboard draw the outlines of a grassy bank, a tree, two rabbits, a bird, and a full moon. Cut them all out.

3

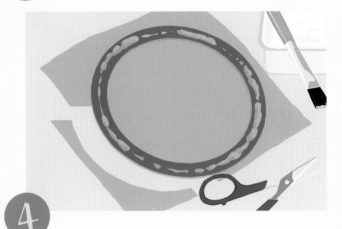

4

Brush glue around one ring and glue the acetate to it, trimming to fit the ring.

Top Tip

Thread some cord through the tab and hang your picture by a window. The sun will shine through it and really make it glow.

5

Glue all the shapes onto the acetate. Cut out a black cardboard tab shape, make a hole in it with the hole punch, and glue it to the top of the black ring. Glue the other black ring on top of the acetate.

Funky friendship bracelet

Tell your best buddy what you think of them with this great friendship bracelet.

1 Take the four strands and knot them together 8 inches from one end.

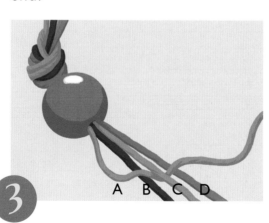

2 Thread the large bead on and push it up as far as the knot.

A B C D

3 Spread out the four strands so that the 2 mauve strands are first and third from the left. Put A over B, under C, and over D. Pull A gently to tighten the weave.

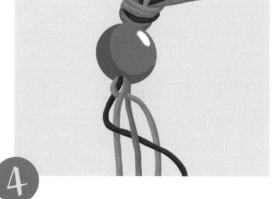

4 Continue weaving the left-hand strand to the right, working over, under, over, under. Pull gently to tighten before starting on the next left-hand strand.

5

Continue weaving until you are about 3 inches from the end, then tie the knotted strands into a knot, leaving the ends loose.

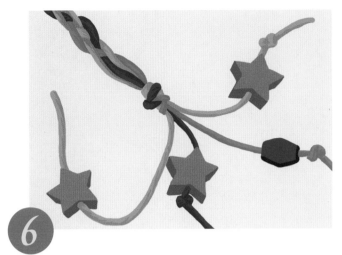

6

Thread a medium-sized bead onto each of the four loose strands and tie a knot to keep in place.

Try This!

Keyring

You can use the same weaving method to make other gifts. This keyring was made with purple and orange strands threaded with pink beads.

Kitty photo album

Making pictures from different shapes and colors of paper is called collage. This collage photo album makes a purr-fect present for your favorite cat lover!

You Will Need

- 6 sheets 11 x 8 inch colored cardboard
- Scraps of card in orange, white, pink, green, black, and blue
- Hole punch
- Pinking shears
- White glue
- 3-foot long piece of green cord

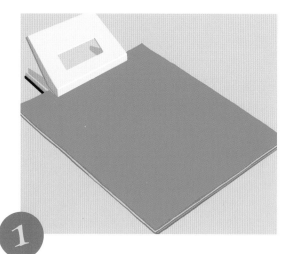

1 Pile together the six sheets of colored cardboard with cover sheet on top. Punch two holes on the left-hand side.

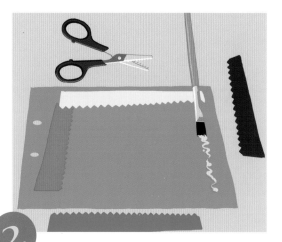

2 Cut a strip each from the card scraps, using the pinking shears. Arrange them to make a border on the cover and glue in place.

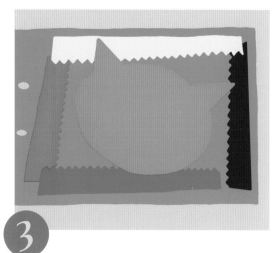

3 Draw and cut out a large cat face from orange cardboard. Stick it on the cover, overlapping the borders as shown.

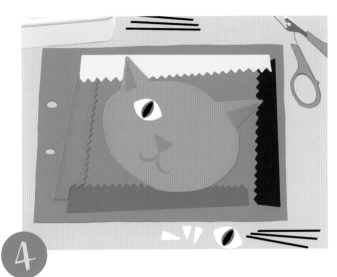

4 Draw and cut out the cat's oval white eyes with green and black pupils. Cut out pink nose, mouth, and ears, and black whiskers. Arrange these on the face and glue them in place.

5 Thread the length of cord through the holes, starting from the back and including all the pages. Tie in a bow at the front. Knot the ends of the cord to stop them from fraying.

Secret book box

Had enough of sneaky sisters or beastly brothers stealing your treasures? This clever box disguised as a book will really fool them!

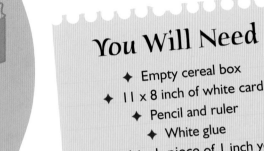

You Will Need

- ✦ Empty cereal box
- ✦ 11 x 8 inch of white card
- ✦ Pencil and ruler
- ✦ White glue
- ✦ 2 ft 6 inch piece of 1 inch yellow ribbon
- ✦ 16 ½ x 11 ¾ inch sheet of light blue foam
- ✦ 11 x 8 inch sheet of dark blue foam

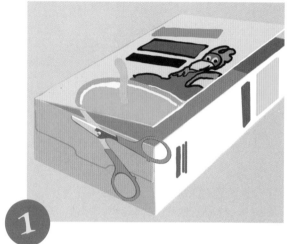

1 Cut the front of the empty box around three sides. Leave the left side uncut so it makes a flap.

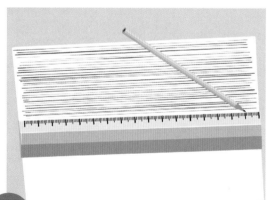

2 Draw straight lines on the white cardboard along the longer side. Using the box as a guide, cut out pieces of the lined cardboard to fit on the top, bottom and side of the box. Glue them in place.

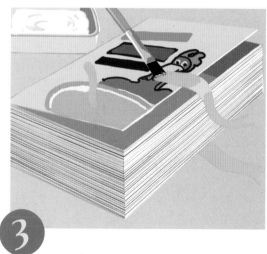

3 Cut the ribbon in half and glue one piece to the back of the box and the other to the front flap, halfway down.

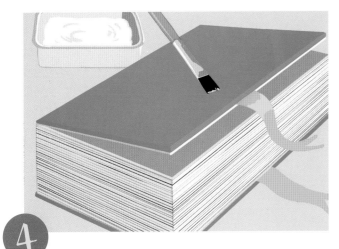

◀ Using the box as a guide, cut two pieces of light blue foam, each a fraction of an inch bigger than the box on all sides. Glue one piece to the front flap and the other to the back.

4

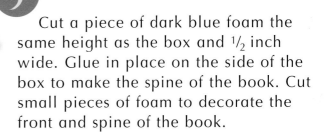

5

Cut a piece of dark blue foam the same height as the box and 1/2 inch wide. Glue in place on the side of the box to make the spine of the book. Cut small pieces of foam to decorate the front and spine of the book.

Top
Tip

Use a marker pen to give your book a boring title so that nobody will open it, such as *How to Tidy Your Bedroom* by A. Mom.

Flowery earrings

It's really easy to make jewelry with oven-bake clay and it comes in so many colors you'll never run out of ideas.

You Will Need

✦ Oven-bake clay: red, yellow, blue
✦ Rolling pin
✦ Plastic sheet or tablecloth
✦ Plastic knife
✦ Earring backs
✦ All-purpose glue

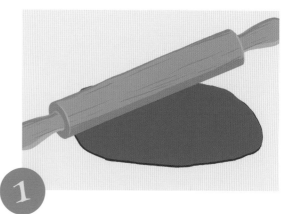

1 Spread out a plastic sheet or old tablecloth to work on. Work the clay in your hands to warm it. Roll out the blue clay until it's almost paper thin.

2 Take half the piece of red clay and roll it into a sausage about ¼ inch in diameter.

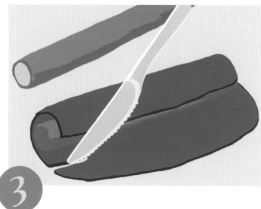

3 Put the red sausage on the blue piece and roll them up together. Now make a red sausage with a yellow middle in the same way.

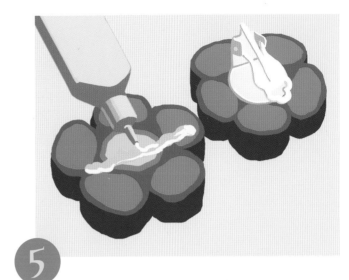

4 Cut the blue sausage into five equal pieces, and cut two equal pieces of the red sausage. Arrange them in a flower shape as shown.

5 Use the plastic knife to slice the shape into two pieces. Bake them in the oven following the manufacturer's instructions. Leave them to cool, then glue the earring backs on.

Try This!

Pretty pendants

Once you get the hang of handling the clay, you can create all kinds of designs. Let your imagination run wild! These drop earrings were made with leftovers from the main project.

Candy mirror

This is a great way to make a boring old mirror more exciting. Instead of soft candies, you could use beads, sequins, or buttons.

You Will Need

♦ Bag of small soft candies

♦ Spray varnish

♦ Toothpicks and lump of modeling clay

♦ White glue and brush

♦ Old mirror

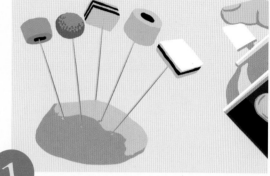

1 Spear the candies on toothpicks sticks stuck in clay. Get an adult to spray them with varnish.

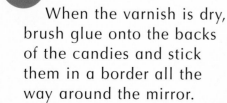

2 When the varnish is dry, brush glue onto the backs of the candies and stick them in a border all the way around the mirror.

MODELING

Dog and kennel

Make a dotty dalmatian from oven-bake clay; then turn an old juice carton into a cozy kennel for him to curl up in.

You Will Need

- ◆ Juice or milk carton
- ◆ Scissors
- ◆ Paintbrush
- ◆ Paints: yellow, red, green
- ◆ Oven bake clay: Black, white, red

1 Cut around the carton about 4 inches from the top. Rinse it and leave to dry.

2 Cut an arched doorway, then paint the kennel yellow, with a red roof. Paint tufts of green grass and a red border around the door.

Dog's dinner

Complete the scene by making your pooch a juicy bone with white clay and a doggy bowl with the red clay.

◄ Use the white clay to make the head and body shapes of the dog. Push the head onto the body, making sure it is firmly attached.

3

4

Make one white and one black ear, and a black patch for the forehead. Now make little sausage shapes for the legs and tail, and add all of them to your model.

5

Stick on black spots and a round nose, one black eye, and one with a black spot in the middle of a white spot. Use red for the collar and tongue. Bake your model according to manufacturer's instructions.

Clay eggcup

This big-footed eggcup is brilliant. Paint a funny face on your boiled egg and make breakfast time really egg-citing!

You Will Need

+ 7 ounces air-drying clay
+ Plastic knife
+ Egg
+ Acrylic paints: blue, red, black
+ Paintbrush

1 Set one-quarter of the clay to one side. Roll the remaining clay into a ball and use your thumbs to work it into a bowl shape. Check the bowl with an egg, working on the shape until the egg sits snugly in the hollow.

2 Divide the remaining clay into two equal pieces. Make a fat foot shape out of each and fix them to the base of the bowl. Score the bowl with a toothpick and wet each piece to help them stick.

3 Turn the model the right way up and adjust the feet until the model stands on a surface without wobbling. Leave to dry overnight.

4
Paint the bowl of the eggcup blue. Paint red socks and black shoes, adding a black line across the socks to make a bar.

Try This!

Stylish sneakers

Use a toothpick to add details to the jeans and small flattened pieces of clay to make tongues for sneakers. Paint the jeans red and blue and the sneakers silver with black laces and toes.

Top Tip
Don't put your eggcup in the dishwasher. Wash it quickly and carefully by hand to keep it looking good as new.

Flying bird mobile

Turn your bedroom into a tropical bird paradise with a colorful mobile. Invisible thread makes it look as if the birds are really flying!

1 Roll out the air-drying clay to about ¹/₄ inch thick.

You Will Need

✦ Package of air-drying clay
✦ Rolling pin
✦ Paper
✦ Plastic knife
✦ Old ballpoint pen
✦ Set of paints, including gold
✦ Paintbrush
✦ 5 colored feathers
✦ Sequins
✦ Colored and invisible thread
✦ 20 inches of wire and pliers

2 ◄ Trace the bird template on p.223 onto a piece of paper and cut it out. Put it on the clay and cut around it with a plastic knife. Repeat until you have made five birds. Use an old pen to make a hole at the top of each bird. Leave to dry.

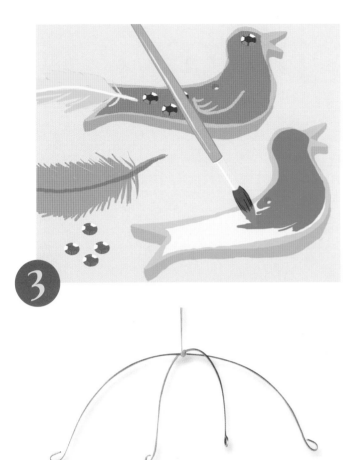

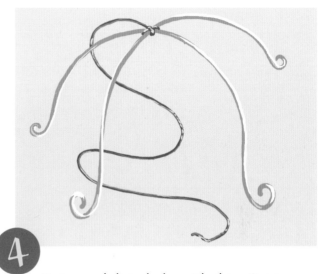

◀ Decorate the birds in acrylic paints, then outline them gold paint and glue on sequins. Glue a feather to each tail.

3

4

Get an adult to help with this. Cut two pieces of wire 10 inches long, and use pliers to make small hooks at the ends. Bend the wires into semicircles. Tie the wires together with a long piece of colored thread.

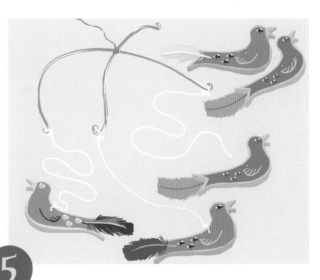

5

Use invisible thread to attach a bird to each hook. Hang the fifth bird from where the two wires join at the center.

Mosaic plate

Make your very own Roman mosaic. Simply make tiles from clay and get designing! Create a spiral like this, or copy a simple drawing you have made.

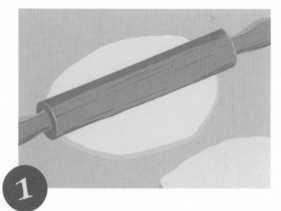

1 Roll out each color of clay to about ¼ inch thick.

You Will Need

- ✦ Old dinner plate
- ✦ Oven-bake clay: white, orange, red, green, blue
- ✦ Plaster of paris
- ✦ Butter knife
- ✦ Rolling pin
- ✦ Plate-hanging hook

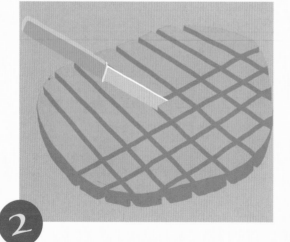

2 Cut all the clay layers into ¼ inch squares. Ask an adult to put the squares in the oven and bake them according to the manufacturer's instructions.

3 Mix some plaster of paris with water in a plastic bowl and smear it all over the plate. Lay out the tiles on a work surface in a spiral pattern.

4

◁ Add the tiles, one color at a time, pushing them into the plaster. Leave the plate to dry overnight.

Wipe the plate with a damp cloth to remove any extra bits of plaster.

Why not hang your plate on the wall for everyone to admire? You can buy plate hanging hooks in hardware stores.

Top Tip
Apply a thin coat of varnish to your plate to make it longer.

119

Brilliant beads

These beads are made from three different colors of clay, but if you only have one color simply make the beads and, when they are dry, paint them instead.

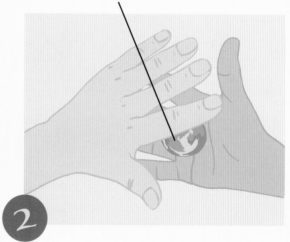

You Will Need

✦ Air-drying clay: green, yellow, turquoise
✦ Darning needle
✦ 15 toothpicks
✦ Thin elastic thread

Make sure you make all the balls the same size!

1 Roll the three colors of clay into sausages and put them side by side. Use a plastic knife to cut sections of about the same size through all three lengths together.

2 Take a section and roll it into a ball between your palms until the colors are mixed together. Repeat until you have made about 15 balls.

Try This!

Square shaped

These square beads are just as easy to make as the round ones. Make little clay balls, then gently flatten each ball on each side between your thumb and forefinger until you have cube shapes.

3 Push a toothpick through the middle of each ball. Balance the sticks across the top of a mug, so that the beads are fully exposed to the air, and leave them to dry. They will be ready in about 24 hours.

4 Use a darning needle to thread the beads onto thin elastic until you have enough to go around your wrist comfortably. Knot the two ends of elastic together and trim the ends.

Papier-mâché CD holder

Granola bar boxes are perfect to make this groovy CD holder, so get munching!

You Will Need

- 4 identical empty cardboard granola bar boxes
- Scissors
- White glue
- Masking tape
- Thick cardboard
- Torn newspaper pieces
- Paints: white, silver
- Brush
- 3 old CDs

1

◁ Cut the lids off of all the boxes. Glue the boxes in a row and add masking tape along the joins.

2

Cut out two squares of thick cardboard the same size as the box sides, and glue one to each end of the boxes.

3

Make papier-mâché mix following the recipe on p6. Apply a layer of newspaper all over the outside and around the edges of the boxes.

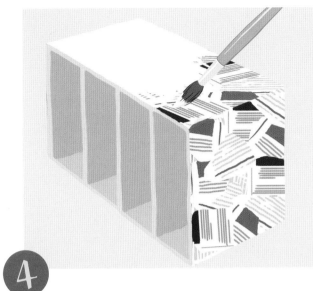

4 When the papier-mâché is dry, paint the boxes white all over. Leave to dry.

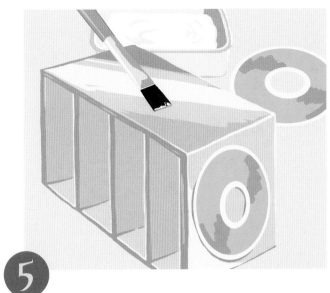

5 Paint the outside silver. When it is dry, glue a CD on each end and on the top.

Scented hangings

Hang these fragrant little butterflies in your clothes chest and your clothing will always smell fresh. They make great gifts, too!

You Will Need

+ Salt-dough mixture
+ Butterfly-shaped cookie cutter
+ Acrylic paints
+ Ribbon
+ Toothpick
+ Rolling pin
+ Baking sheet
+ Lavender essential oil

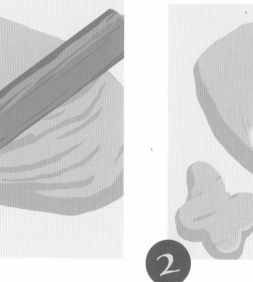

1 Make the salt dough, using the recipe on p.6. Roll it out to a thickness of about ³/₄ inch.

2 Use a cookie cutter to cut shapes out of the dough. Make a hole at the top of each shape with the toothpick.

3 Ask an adult to help here. Put the shapes on a cookie sheet and bake as in the recipe on p.6. Leave to cool.

4 Paint the shapes, leaving a small square on the back unpainted.

Top Tip Lavender oil is said to help you sleep, so hang a butterfly over your bed. You'll soon be having sweet dreams!

5 Add a few drops of lavender essential oil to the unpainted area. Thread a ribbon through the hole and knot it at the back.

Try This!

Valentine's gift
Heart-shaped hangings make a great Valentine's day gift for a special friend!

Mini farmyard

Make your own farmyard scene of cute sheep and clucking chickens with oven-drying clay. Ask an adult to help you bake them.

You Will Need

◆ Oven-drying clay: brown, red, yellow, white, black, green

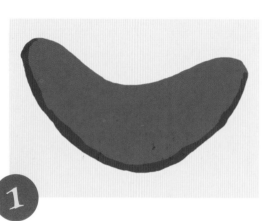

1 For the hens, mold the brown clay into simple crescent shapes.

2 Stick a lump of red at one end for the comb, and a tiny red one underneath for the wattle. Add a yellow beak.

3 Add small black blobs for eyes. Mount the hen on a flattened green blob and push it down well.

4 For the sheep, mold white clay into an oval shape for the body. Make a head, two ears, and four legs out of the black clay.

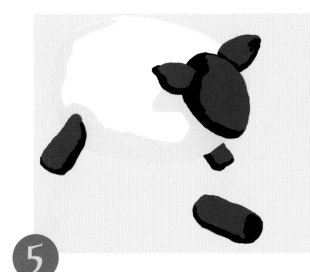

5 Stick the head, ears, and legs to the sheep's body. Wet the clay slightly to make it stick better. Bake all the animals in the oven, following the manufacturer's instructions.

Papier-mâché bowl

Balloons are great for making bowls. After the papier-mâché dries, just pop the balloon to leave a perfect bowl shape!

You Will Need

+ Balloon
+ Torn newspaper pieces
+ White glue and water
+ Scissors
+ Masking tape
+ Round plastic bendy lid
+ White latex paint and brush
+ Ruler and pencil
+ Set of acrylic paints
+ Water-based varnish and brush

1 Blow up the balloon. Make the papier-mâché mix using the recipe on p.7. Paste a layer of newspaper strips halfway up the balloon. Repeat with three more layers.

2 When it is dry, pop the balloon and remove it. Trim the edges of the bowl by cutting around the rim.

3 Sit the bowl in the plastic lid and tape them together. Paste two more layers of papier-mâché over the whole model and leave it to dry.

4 Paint the pot all over, including the inside, with a coat of white latex paint. Leave to dry. Hold the ruler up beside the pot and mark two straight lines of dots around the bowl. Join the dots to make lines.

5 Paint on a striped pattern in bright colors and leave to dry. Add spots, triangles, and black outlines. Leave to dry, then add a thin coat of varnish to make the bowl tough and shiny.

Copy this colorful design or make up a pattern of your own.

Top Tip It's important to leave papier-mâché to dry before you pop the balloon or start painting. If it is still soft and damp, you could easily put your finger through it!

Farmyard barn

Don't forget to save all your old cardboard boxes. You can use them to make this handy barn for your farmyard toys.

You Will Need

✦ Plain and corrugated cardboard
✦ Scissors
✦ Pencil and ruler
✦ Brush and white glue
✦ Green and pink tissue paper
✦ Paints: cream, brown, dark brown, orange

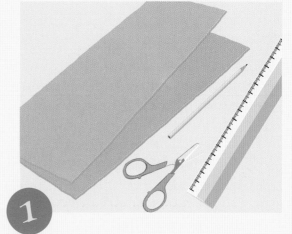

1 Cut out two pieces of cardboard measuring 10 x 4 inches. These will be the base and back of the barn.

2 Now cut two more rectangles measuring 4 x 6 inches. Put them on top of each other and cut the corners off to make a roof shape. Glue all four pieces together and leave to dry.

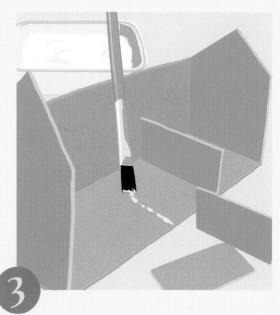

3 Cut three rectangles measuring 2 ³/₄ x 4 inches to make the stalls. Glue them in place and leave to dry.

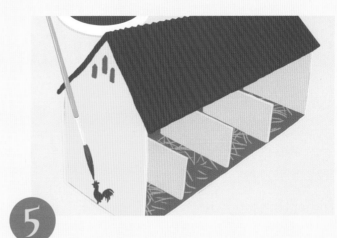

4 Cut a rectangle measuring 8 x 10 inches from the corrugated cardboard. Make a crease by folding in half lengthways, then put it on top of the barn and glue it in place.

5 Paint the roof brown and the rest of the barn creamy white. Put windows and a chicken on the side in dark brown. Paint the floor brown and add some straw in orange.

Top Tip Corrugated cardboard is often used to package furniture or electrical goods, so keep an eye out for it.

6 When the paint has dried, make flowers and leaves by scrunching up scraps of tissue paper and gluing them to the side of the barn.

Photo-frame fridge magnet

This fridge magnet is designed to look like a dog's collar. It's perfect for showing off a photo of your favorite mutt!

1

Roll out a piece of red clay into a sausage shape about 3/4 inch thick and 4 inches long. Make the shape into a circle, overlapping the edges and pressing them together gently with your fingers.

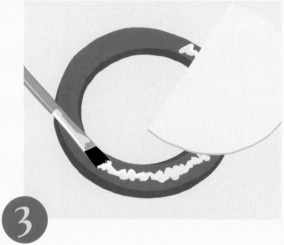

2

Add a buckle and a name tag in yellow clay. Use a pencil to make holes in the collar. Put the shape on a cookie sheet and bake according to the manufacturer's instructions.

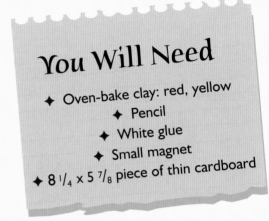

3

Cut a circle of thin cardboard slightly smaller than the frame. Cut off the top third of the circle. Brush glue around the frame and stick the cardboard to it to make a pocket.

4 Trim your dog photo so that it will fit in the frame. Slip it into the pocket.

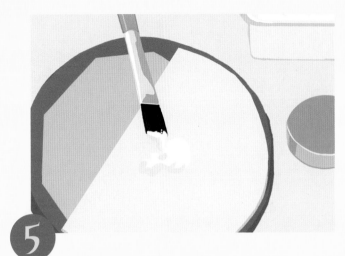

5 Glue a magnet onto the back of the frame and leave it to dry.

Try This!

You've been framed!

Design a frame and put a picture of yourself in it. Now all you need to do is find someone who'd like to see your smiling face on their fridge every day!

Flowerpot pups

Get cracking with air-drying clay to make this doggy flowerpot. With his huge eyes and floppy tongue, he looks barking mad!

You Will Need

✦ Flowerpot, 3 ½ inches diameter
✦ Air-drying clay
✦ Toothpick
✦ Plastic knife
✦ Brown acrylic paint and paint brush
✦ Tube of gold paint

1 Roll a ball of clay about 1½ inches in diameter. Cut into the ball and pull it gently apart to make the dog's jowls. Wet one side with your fingers and fix to the center of the pot. Prick each side with a toothpick.

Top Tip Speed up the drying process by putting your pot in a warm, dry place.

2 Roll a small ball of clay for the nose and stick it on top of the jowls. Make holes in it for nostrils. Stick on a tongue shape and two round eyes, with smaller balls for the eyeballs.

3 For the ears, make 2 tapered ovals about 3 inches long. Use the knife to dab marks all over them. Attach them on each side by wetting and smoothing them onto the surface, leaving the loose ends to hang over the side. Leave to dry overnight.

4 Paint the pot all over with the brown acrylic paint. Leave to dry. Use your finger to rub small amounts of gold paint over the pot, so it gleams in the light.

Try This!

Family of pots

Create a whole family of different dog pots! This miniature pup is painted red and was made with a 2 inch pot.

Slithery snail pots

These smiling snails look great and they have a useful secret. You can hide your tiny treasures under their shell!

You Will Need

- ✦ 5 ounces air-drying clay
- ✦ Plastic knife
- ✦ Purple pipe cleaner
- ✦ Toothpick
- ✦ Acrylic paints: red, blue, yellow, purple, black, white
- ✦ Paintbrush

1 Cut the clay in half. From one half take enough to roll a ¾ inch ball of clay and two tiny balls. Stick the two tiny balls on the ¾ inch ball for the eyes, flattening them as you attach them. Cut two pieces of pipe cleaner and poke them into the head.

2 With the rest of the clay from the first half, make a tapered oval shape. Use your thumbs to indent it a little in the middle. Stick the head to the untapered end.

◄ Roll the other half of clay into a ball. Use your thumbs to shape the ball into a hollow snail's shell shape. Make sure the shape fits the base of your model. Add a spiral on each side using the toothpick. Leave all the pieces to dry overnight.

3

4

Paint the the head purple, the eyes white, and the base blue.

Try This!

Spotted grasshopper

For a grasshopper pot, make a long base and lid and push green pipe-cleaner legs into the base. Paint the pot bright green all over and add red spots.

5

Paint the shell yellow and red and pick out the spiral with black paint. Using the black paint, add a smiling mouth and paint on pupils for the eyes.

137

Lighthouse

Ahoy there, landlubbers! To make this model lighthouse project even easier, you can use ready-mixed filler—buy it in a hardware store.

1

Turn the yogurt carton upside down and tape it to the upturned lid.

You Will Need

✦ 18 ounces plaster of paris
✦ Water
✦ Shoe box lid
✦ Yogurt carton
✦ Clear adhesive
✦ Plastic knife
✦ Old plastic mixing container
✦ About 20 small pebbles
✦ Air-drying clay
✦ Acrylic paints: blue, white, green, brown, black
✦ All-purpose glue

Make the surface rough so it looks like a choppy sea.

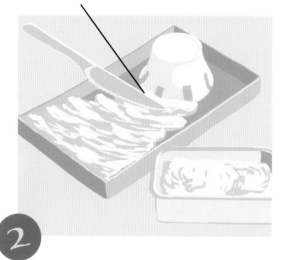

2

Mix the plaster of paris with water in a plastic container until it is thick and sticky. Spread the mixture all over the base with a plastic knife.

3

Now coat the yogurt carton with the plaster and push small pebbles around the base of the carton to look like rocks. Leave it to dry.

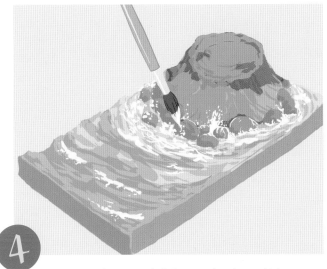

4 Remove the model from the box lid. Paint the island green and brown and the sea blue with white flecks, blending the colors for a realistic effect.

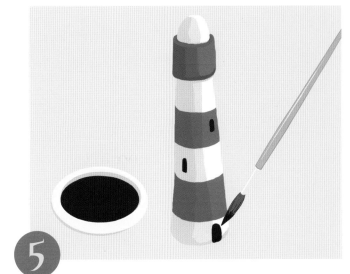

5 Now for the lighthouse. Roll a tapering tube about 4 inches long from the clay, and add a strip around the top of the tower. When the clay is dry, paint it red and white, with a few black windows and a door.

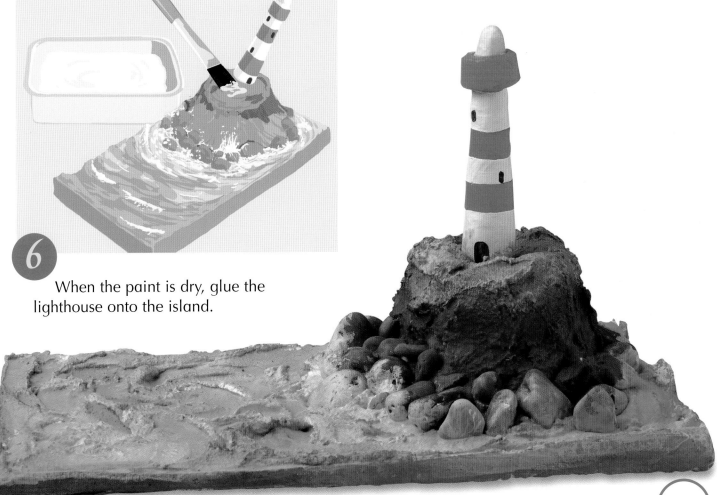

6 When the paint is dry, glue the lighthouse onto the island.

GET MODELING

Salt-dough basket

If you don't have any clay, you can create your own! Salt dough is cheap and easy to make and can be used for all kinds of modeling projects.

You Will Need

✦ Salt dough mixture (see p.7)
✦ Flour
✦ Rolling pin and plastic knife
✦ Kitchen foil
✦ Shallow ovenproof dish
✦ Old ballpoint pen
✦ Paints: blue, red, green and brush
✦ Small scrap of green felt
✦ Scissors
✦ All-purpose glue

1 Sprinkle flour on the salt dough and roll it out to about $^3/_4$ inch thick. Use a plastic knife to cut 15 strips.

2 Cover the inside of a dish with kitchen foil. Lay a line of strips across the bowl. Now weave a strip down the middle of the bowl in the opposite direction.

3 Carry on weaving strips to make a basket. Press a thin strip of dough all around the rim. Make strawberries from leftover dough, then poke holes in them with an old pen.

4 Bake the basket and fruit in the oven according to the instructions on p.7. When they are cold, separate the dish from the basket. Paint the basket blue and the strawberries red with green dots.

5 Cut stalk shapes from the green felt and glue them to the tops of the strawberries. Then glue the strawberries to the edge of the basket.

Sheriff's badge

Make some salt dough, model yourself a lawman's badge, and run those baddies out of town!

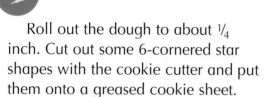

1 Roll out the dough to about ¼ inch. Cut out some 6-cornered star shapes with the cookie cutter and put them onto a greased cookie sheet.

You Will Need

- Salt dough (see recipe on p.7 and use half the amounts)
- 6-cornered star cookie cutter
- Cookie sheet, greased
- Brooch backs
- All-purpose glue
- Silver paint and brush

2 Roll six tiny balls. Wet the corners of the stars and stick a ball on each corner. Bake according to the recipe on p.7. Then paint the star silver. Leave to dry, then glue a brooch back to the star.

TOYS and GAMES

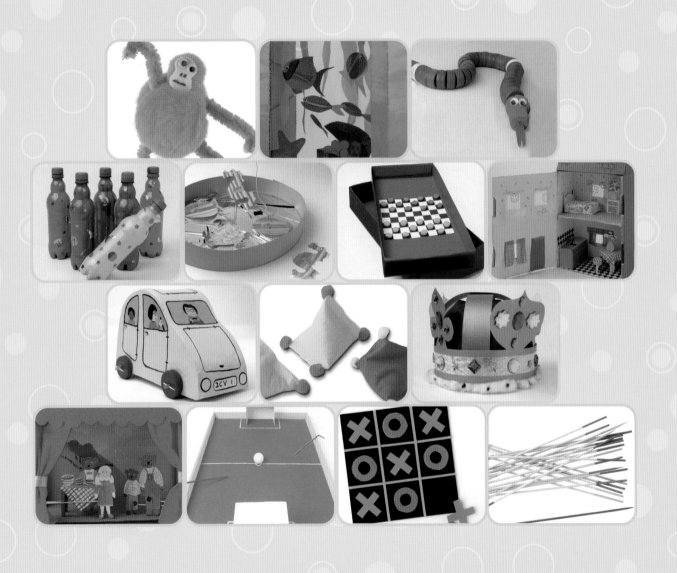

Funky monkeys

This pair of acrobatic monkeys love just hanging around with each other! They are made from bendy pipe cleaners and fluffy pompoms.

You Will Need

- ✦ 3 x 12 inch brown chenille pipe cleaners
- ✦ White glue
- ✦ 4 x 2 inch pompoms
- ✦ 2 x 1 inch pompoms
- ✦ Scrap of beige felt
- ✦ Black fine marker pen
- ✦ 4 tiny goggle eyes

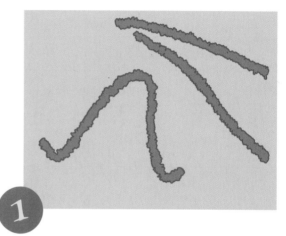

1 Cut the pipe cleaners in half to make 6 equal pieces. Bend one piece in half to make the legs, then bend the ends to make feet. Repeat with another piece for the arms and hands.

2 To make the tail, fix another pipe cleaner to the center of the legs and arms, winding the end around at the bends to join them all together.

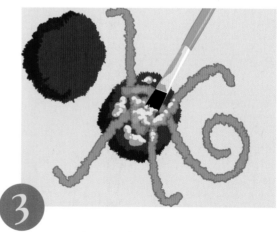

3 Use white glue to stick two of the larger pompoms together, sandwiching the legs, arms, and tail between them.

4

To make a head, cut a small figure-eight shape from the felt. Glue goggle eyes on the felt face and use the marker to draw nostrils and a mouth. Glue the face to a 1 inch pompom.

5

Glue the head to the top of the pompom body and leave it to dry. Bend the arms, legs, and tail into shape. Repeat for the second monkey.

Try This!

Creepy crawly

This terrifying tarantula is made from four pipe cleaners for the legs, with two pompoms holding them in place. Add eyes, antennas, and a hungry mouth and he'll give your friends the shivers!

Shoe-box aquarium

Make your own seabed scene, complete with a chest full of sunken treasures. The best thing about these fish is they don't need feeding!

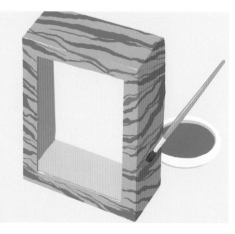

You Will Need

+ Empty shoe box
+ Set of paints
+ Scissors
+ Blue acetate film
+ Clear adhesive tape
+ White paper and pencil
+ Clear thread
+ Tissue paper: light and dark green

1 Cut the bottom out of the box, leaving a 3/4 inch border all around.

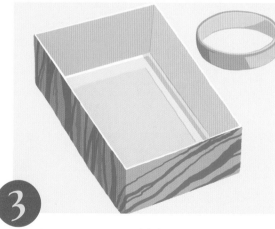

2 Paint the box light blue all over except for the floor. When it is dry, paint a few light green and darker blue streaks over it. Paint the floor sandy yellow.

3 Cut a piece of blue acetate film to fit inside the window. Stick it in place with tape.

4
On white paper, draw and color in different fish, a starfish, and a treasure chest on a mound of brown sand. Cut them out.

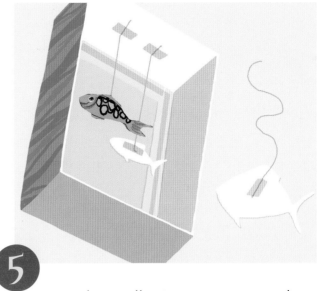

5
Use clear adhesive tape to attach clear thread to the fish and tape the other ends to the box top, so the fish look as if they are swimming.

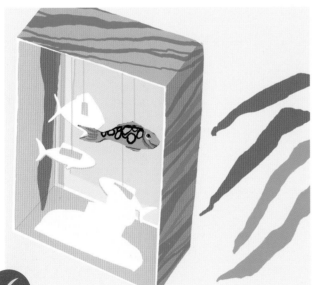

6
Cut four strips from the tissue paper and tape them to the top of the box so they hang down like seaweed. Tape the starfish to the side of the box. Fold down the bottom of the treasure chest and tape the flap to the floor.

Bottle-top snake

Use the tops of plastic soft-drinks bottles to make a super, slithery snake. Ask an adult to save you the two wine corks you need.

You Will Need

- ✦ Champagne-style cork
- ✦ Wine cork
- ✦ Green acrylic paint and brush
- ✦ Plastic bottle tops: 30 green, a few red and white
- ✦ Old ballpoint pen
- ✦ 3 small screw eyes
- ✦ 24 inch piece of string
- ✦ Small bell
- ✦ 2 goggle eyes
- ✦ Scrap of red felt
- ✦ Scissors
- ✦ White glue

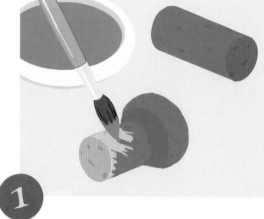

1 Paint the two corks all over with the green acrylic paint. Leave to dry.

2 Using the old ballpoint pen, make a hole in the middle of each of the bottle tops.

3 Screw one eye into the top of the champagne cork. Add the bell to another screw eye, and screw this and the remaining eye into each end of the wine cork.

4 Thread one end of the string through the bottom of a green bottle top. Now thread it though the champagne cork eye and back through the bottle top. Make a knot and trim one end only.

5 Thread all the bottle tops onto the string, keeping them all facing the same way around. Finish by tying the string to the screw eye on the wine cork.

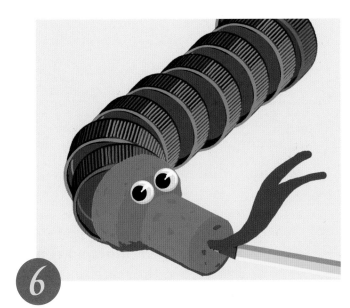

6

◀ Glue the two goggle eyes in place. Cut a thin forked tongue from the red felt and use the pen to poke it into the cork.

149

Bottle skittles

Play skittles in the backyard or, if it's raining, indoors. But don't play anywhere near the best china!

You Will Need

✦ 6 identical clear plastic drinks bottles with lids
✦ Ready-mixed paints: red, yellow, green
✦ Dishwashing liquid
✦ Old jug
✦ Self-adhesive star and planet stickers
✦ Funnel
✦ Sand

1 In an old jug, mix the green paint with water until it looks like thin custard. Add a small squirt of dishwashing liquid.

2 Pour some paint mixture into a bottle and put the top on. Shake the bottle to spread the paint all over the inside of the bottle. Add more paint if you need to, until the whole inside is covered.

3 Remove the top, pour out any remaining paint and leave the bottle to dry. Repeat for the other bottles, making three red, two green, and one yellow bottle.

◄ Put the funnel in the neck of a bottle and pour in sand to about halfway. This makes the skittles harder to knock over. Repeat for each of the bottles.

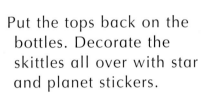

Put the tops back on the bottles. Decorate the skittles all over with star and planet stickers.

Top Tip

Painting the skittles from the inside of the bottle means the paint won't chip when you play with them.

Fishing game

Challenge your friends to a game of magnetic fishing and see who can land the best catch!

You Will Need

- ◆ Sheets of white paper
- ◆ Pencil and scissors
- ◆ Set of paints and brush
- ◆ Foil paper
- ◆ Thick cardboard
- ◆ Sheet of blue card
- ◆ Clear adhesive tape
- ◆ Paperclips
- ◆ 2 garden stakes and string
- ◆ Magnets and hole punch
- ◆ White glue

1 Draw a fish, a crab, and a seahorse. Cut them out and draw round them to make more. Make four fish, four crabs and two seahorses in total.

2 Use bright-colored paints to decorate the creatures and add eyes to the seahorses and fish. Glue colored paper on the fish to make fins.

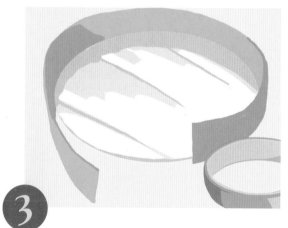

3 Cut 14 inch ovals of cardboard and foil and glue them together. Cut a strip of blue cardboard about 43 x 1½ inches and put it around the card to make the rim of the pool. Tape the ends of the strip together.

Put all the creatures in the pool and take turns to fish them out. When all have been caught, add up the numbers on the bottoms. The winner is the person with the highest score!

4 Write the following numbers on the bottoms of the creatures: 2 on the fish; 5 on the crabs; and 10 on the seahorses. Attach a paperclip to each creature.

5 Make two fishing rods by tying magnets to two garden stakes with string. Use thin, flexible magnets that are used for making fridge magnets. An ordinary hole punch will make a hole in these for the string.

153

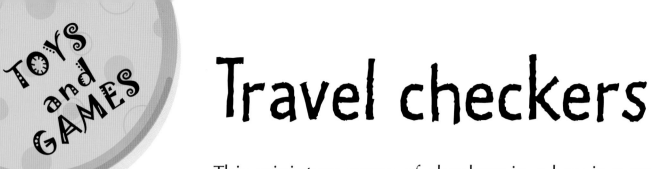
Travel checkers

This miniature game of checkers in a box is a great way to keep you and your friends from getting bored on long car or train journeys.

You Will Need

- ✦ Shoe box
- ✦ Paints: red, white, blue
- ✦ Paintbrush
- ✦ White glue
- ✦ Ruler and pencil
- ✦ Sheets of paper: 1 white, 1 blue
- ✦ Scissors
- ✦ Oven-bake clay: green and yellow
- ✦ Plastic knife

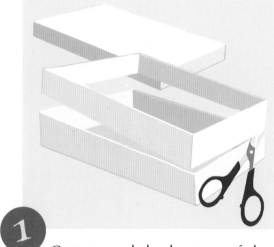

1 Cut around the bottom of the shoe box to make a tray about 2 inches deep.

2 Paint the lid and the tray red all over. You might need to do two coats to cover all the lettering.

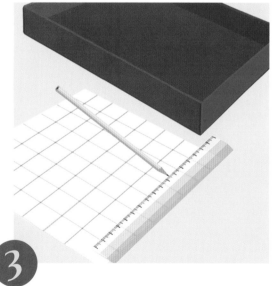

3 Measure the width of the tray and cut your paper into a square the same size. Draw a grid on the paper of 8 x 8 squares.

4 Make a grid exactly the same size on the blue paper. Cut out the blue squares and stick them onto the white grid, so that every other square is blue.

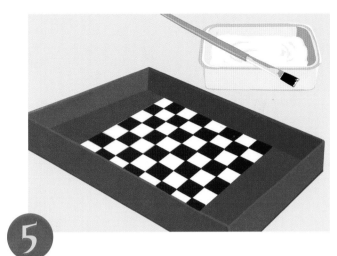

5 Spread white glue on the back of the paper and stick it down inside the box.

6 ◄ Roll each piece of clay into a sausage shape and use the plastic knife to slice each one into 12 disks. Bake them according to the manufacturer's instructions.

Doll's house

Make your dolls a stylish new home. Although there are lots of steps, it's really simple to do. Turn the page to see the doll's house opened up.

You Will Need

✦ Sneakers box with attached lid and sheets of thick cardboard
✦ 3 11 x 8 inch sheets of thin white cardboard
✦ Craft knife
✦ White glue
✦ Scissors
✦ Set of acrylic paints
✦ Colored paper: black, cream
✦ Different scraps of fabric
✦ Sheet of tracing paper
✦ Small boxes and packages
✦ Tin foil
✦ 2 map pins

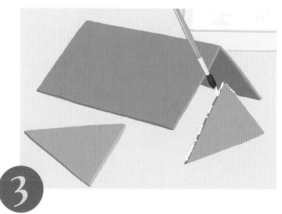

1 Cut a rectangle of thick cardboard the same depth as the box and 1½ inches wider. Fold ¾ inch flaps on each side and glue them inside the box to make a floor.

2 Draw three windows and a door on the box lid. Ask an adult to cut them out, using a craft knife. Only cut around three sides of the door shape, so it opens and closes.

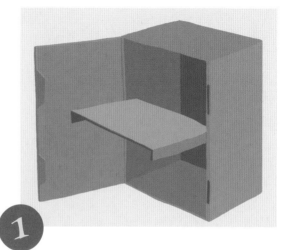

3 Cut a piece of thick cardboard the same width as the box and twice the depth. Fold it in half. Cut out card triangles and glue them to each end to make the roof.

◁ Glue the roof to the house. Paint the outside of the house and the roof brown all over. When it is dry, use white to paint bricks on the walls. Paint around the windows and door. Add a climbing plant.

4

5

Decorate the bedroom. Use pink paint for the walls and add little dots with a dry brush to make wallpaper.

6

Glue a piece of fabric to the bedroom floor for a carpet. For the kitchen floor and splashback, glue little squares of black and cream paper to look like tiles.

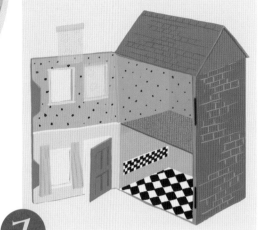

7

◀ Cut small rectangles of fabric for the downstairs curtains and glue them to the tops of the windows. Draw patterns on tracing paper for blinds and tape them to the upstairs windows.

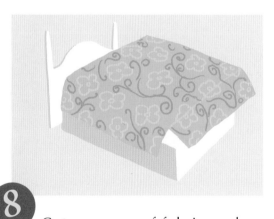

8

Cut a square of fabric and glue it to a small box to make a bed. Cut a headboard out of thin white cardboard and glue to the end of the bed.

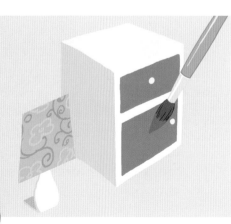

9

◀ Paint another small box brown and white to make a cabinet. Draw a lamp shape, with a small tab at the bottom, on the white cardboard. Glue on a shade made from a scrap of fabric, then glue the tab to the cabinet.

10

For the table, draw around a small jar lid onto white cardboard. Cut it out and glue on a strip of cardboard all around it. Glue on three card legs, then glue on a square of fabric for a tablecloth. Draw a vase of flowers on the cardboard, with a tab at the bottom. Cut it out and glue it to the table top.

11

For the kitchen sink, paint a small box blue and draw on details for cupboards and drawers. Cut a hole for the sink in the top, and glue tin foil along the top, cutting a hole for the sink. Make grooves in the foil with a pencil. Stick two map pins in it for faucets. Glue the sink to the kitchen wall.

Cardboard car

Vroom! This car has proper wheels, so it will whizz along a smooth surface. You can use the card from an empty cereal box to make the body of the car.

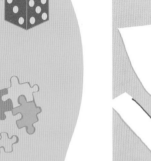

1 Use the template on p.223 to trace two side views of the car. Cut them out. Cut out a rectangle 5 inches wide and 17 inches long.

You Will Need

- ✦ Sheet of cardboard
- ✦ Scissors
- ✦ Masking tape
- ✦ Papier-mâché paste (see p.6)
- ✦ Old newspaper
- ✦ Sandpaper
- ✦ Set of paints and paintbrush
- ✦ 4 plastic bottle tops
- ✦ 2 straws
- ✦ 2 toothpicks

2 Snip out small V shapes 2 inches in from the ends of each side on both pieces of the car.

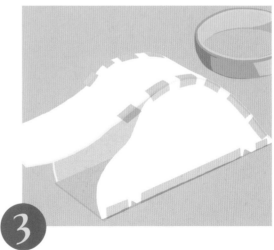

3 Tape all the pieces together. Cut a rectangle of cardboard to fit the base of the car and tape it on too.

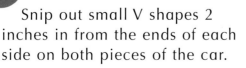

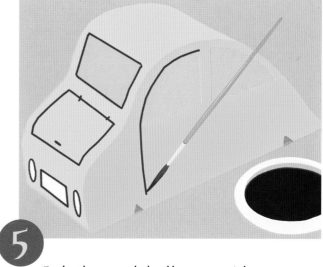

4 Mix up some papier-mâché paste (see p.6) and tear up some newspaper. Cover the car in two layers of paper. Leave the model to dry.

5 Rub the model all over with sandpaper. Paint your car yellow, then add windows, doors, a license plate, headlights, a driver, and a passenger.

6 For wheels, make a hole in each bottle top. Push a straw through the hole and fix it with a small piece of a toothpick. Push the straw through to the other side, trim it to fit, and add the other wheel. Repeat for the back wheels.

2CV 1

Juggling balls

These felt juggling balls are really quick and easy to make, leaving you plenty of time to practice your circus skills. You'll soon be a juggling genius!

You Will Need

✦ 3 felt rectangles:
3 x 6 inches in size 2 yellow, 1 red,
✦ White glue
✦ Scissors
✦ Small dried beans
(i.e. mung beans) or lentils
✦ Spoon
✦ Pompoms: 4 yellow, 8 red
✦ Red and yellow thread and needle

Fold the felt in half here.

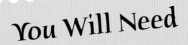

1 Take each felt rectangle and spread glue along one of the longer edges and along one of the shorter edges. Fold it in half and leave it until the glue dries.

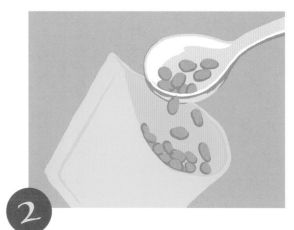

2 Use a spoon to fill the felt bag about two-thirds full with the beans or lentils.

Try This!

Pyramid cushion

If you don't see yourself juggling, make an Egyptian pyramid-shaped cushion instead. Start with a rectangle measuring 12 x 20 inches and use hollow filling instead of beans.

Top Tip

If you want your juggling balls to be extra tough, sew around the seam of each ball after you have glued it.

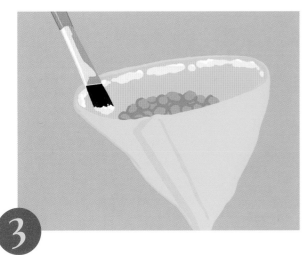

3 Glue along the top of the bag and press the two sides together. Make sure the seam is in the middle of one side, to make a pyramid shape.

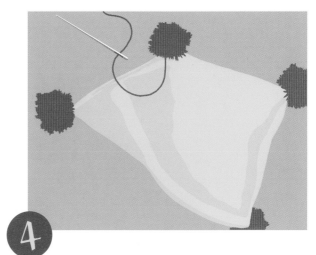

4 Using the needle and thread, sew a pompom onto each of the four corners of the juggling balls.

163

TOYS and GAMES

Royal crown

Make a jeweled crown. Then decide, will
you be a merry monarch or a rotten ruler?

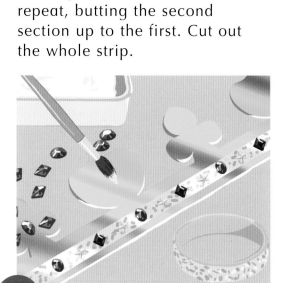

You Will Need

✦ Strip of gold cardboard 5 x 24
inches
✦ 11 x 8 inch tracing paper and
pencil
✦ Scissors and white glue
✦ Hologram film, 1 x 24 inches
✦ 2 strips of gold cardboard 1½ x 13
inches
✦ Paperclips and paper fastener
✦ Purple felt
✦ Large round plate
✦ Cotton batting
✦ Black paint and fine brush

1 Trace the the crown template on
p.222. Transfer it onto the back
of the gold cardboard, then
repeat, butting the second
section up to the first. Cut out
the whole strip.

2 Glue the hologram film along
the base, then glue gems along it
and on the tops. Glue the two
ends to fit loosely on your head,
holding in place with paperclips.

Push a paper fastener through
where the strips meet.

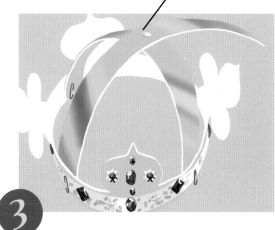

3 Make a mark halfway between
the shapes. Glue the ends of the
short gold strips over the marks.
Hold them in place with
paperclips while they dry.

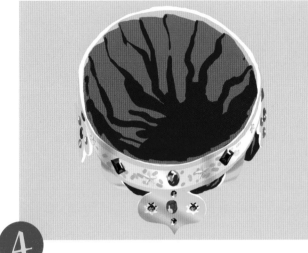

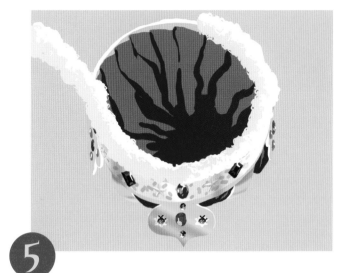

4 Trace around a dinner plate and cut out a circle of purple felt. Make small snips all around the outside of the circle. Put it inside the crown and glue to the inner brim, gluing bit by bit along the clipped edge.

5 Cut a strip of cotton batting about 2 inches wide. Glue it all along the bottom edge of the crown. Paint black spots about 1 inch apart along the length of the cotton batting.

Try This!

Top tiara

Make a simple tiara, cut out with pinking shears. Draw around a dinner plate onto the gold cardboard, then cut it in half and glue it to a simple headband. Decorate the tiara with shiny foil and stick-on jewels.

Miniature theater

There's no need to be bored on a rainy day. Make a shoe-box theater and get your friends to help you put on shows of your favorite stories.

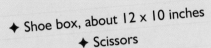

You Will Need

- Shoe box, about 12 x 10 inches
- Scissors
- Pencil, paints and brush
- White glue
- 1 yard red fabric
- Gold ribbon
- Wooden skewers
- Clear adhesive tape
- White paper
- Small square box i.e raisin box

1 Turn the box lengthways and cut a window in each side.

2 Draw a country scene of hills, sheep, and a blue sky with fluffy clouds on the back and sides. Color the scene with paints.

3 Cut two pieces of red fabric 16 x 8 inches. Glue them to the front of the box and decorate with gold ribbon. Cut a strip of fabric 31 inches long and cut one edge into a scalloped shape. Glue it along the top.

4

Draw a picture of Goldilocks and the Three Bears onto thick white paper. Paint them and leave them to dry.

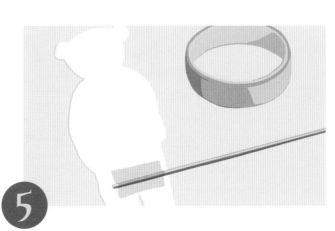

5

Cut out the characters and tape a wooden skewer to the back of each, near their feet.

6

◀ Make a table by cutting into a small cardboard package. Draw a blue checked tablecloth, cut it out, and glue it to the table. Draw three porridge bowls and cut them out, leaving little tabs to stick them to the table.

Blow soccer

If you've got plenty of puff, try a lung-busting game of blow soccer. You can only move the ball by blowing through the straw—no hands allowed!

You Will Need

- ✦ Sheet of cardboard 28 x 20 inches
- ✦ Green felt 35 x 28 inches
- ✦ Clear adhesive tape
- ✦ Wood glue
- ✦ Wood batons: 2 x 28 inches, 2 x 20 inches
- ✦ Acrylic paints: yellow, white
- ✦ Scissors
- ✦ Small cardboard box
- ✦ Red paper
- ✦ 4 toothpicks
- ✦ Drinking straws and ping-pong ball

1 Cover the cardboard with the green felt, pull it tight, and tape it at the back.

You can use chalk for the lines, but you'll have to redraw the lines because it wears off quickly.

2 Turn it over and draw soccer field markings lightly in pencil. Paint over the lines in white.

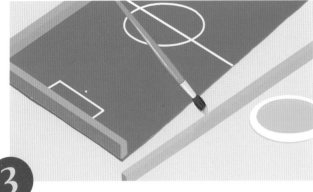

3 Paint the wood batons yellow and glue them together to make a fence around the field.

4 Cut a small cardbord box in half to make goals.

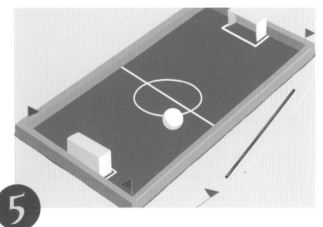

5 Put the goals inside the white boxes on the field. Cut out four small paper triangles and glue them to toothpicks to make corner flags.

Top Tip Play a variation of the game with 10 colored balls, 5 of each color. The winner is the one who blows all their balls into the goal first.

Tic-tac-toe game

Be green and save paper by making a tic-tac-toe game you can use over and over again!

You Will Need

✦ Foam: 1 sheet each in black, orange, purple, and green
✦ Sheet of thick cardboard 8 inches square
✦ Ruler
✦ Scissors
✦ White glue and brush
✦ Paper and pencil

1 Cut an 8 inch square of black funky foam and glue it to the sheet of thick cardboard.

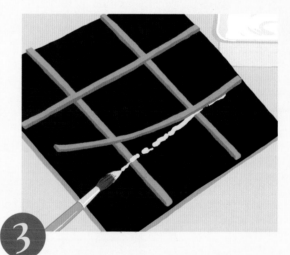

3 Glue the four strips of orange foam to the black foam in a crisscross shape. You can use the ruler to help you position them evenly.

2 Use the ruler and pencil to draw four strips on the orange foam, 8 inches long and about ¼ inch wide. Cut them out.

170

4 Cut the green funky foam in half and glue the halves together to make a double-thick sheet. Repeat with the purple foam.

5 Draw a large X and an 0 onto paper. Cut the shapes out and trace them onto the foam. Make five green Xs and five purple 0s. Cut out the shapes, and you're ready to play!

Try This!

Shells and buttons
Instead of making your 0s and Xs, use shells and buttons to play with.

Pickup sticks

To win this game you'll need a steady hand and nerves of steel. Be careful though—one false move and you'll be out!

You Will Need

✦ 25 wooden sticks
✦ Acrylic paints: red, orange, green, blue, purple
✦ Thin paintbrush
✦ Ruler and pencil

1 Line up six sticks in a row. Use a pencil and ruler to mark each stick 1½ inches from the end.

2 Paint the ends of the six sticks red up to the marks you made. Make orange, green, and blue sets in the same way. Paint the last stick purple all over.

How to play

Drop all the sticks except the purple one in a random heap. Each player takes a turn to try to remove sticks from the pile, one by one, using the purple stick to help. You must only touch the stick you are aiming for—move any others and your turn is over! The player who removes the most sticks is the winner.

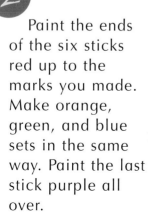

SPECIAL OCCASIONS

Easter chick card

Take a break from devouring your chocolate bunny to make a popup card. Chicks are traditional symbols of Easter. This one is so cute!

You Will Need

✦ 11 x 8 inch sheet of white cardboard
✦ 11 x 8 inch sheet of orange cardboard
✦ Scissors
✦ White glue
✦ Pencil
✦ Felt-tipped pens or coloring pencils
✦ Sheet of yellow paper

1 Fold both sheets of cardboard in half. Cut a 2¼ inch slit in the white card in the center of the folded sheet, at right angles to the fold.

2 Carefully fold in both edges of the slit and make creases so that when you open and close the card, a beak shape pops out.

3 Draw a large, round chick's body around the beak shape. Use scribbly strokes to make your chick look fluffy.

4

Draw black eyes and legs on the body. Cut two wing shapes from the yellow paper and glue them to the body. Make sure the wings stay inside the edges of the card.

5

Paste glue over the back of the white card, avoiding the beak part. Stick it to the orange card, and write "Happy Easter" on the front of the card.

Try This!

Groovy chicks

Make a three-chick version by folding the card lengthways and cutting three slits for beaks.

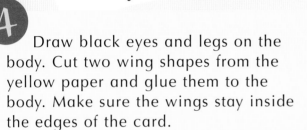

Chinese dragon

Dragons are symbols of good fortune in Chinese New Year celebrations. Maybe this colorful dragon will bring you luck, so keep your fingers crossed!

You Will Need

+ 11 x 8 inch colored paper: red, yellow, green
  + Scissors
  + White glue
  + Clear adhesive tape
+ Tissue paper: pink and white
  + Pencil
+ Paints: Black, red, yellow, gold, white
  + Paintbrush
  + Thick white paper
  + Garden stakes

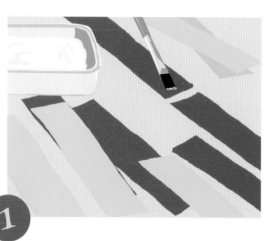

1 Cut the paper into 1½ inch wide strips and glue them together until you have two strips, each about 47 inches long.

2 Glue the two strips together at one end at right angles to each other. Put one strip over the other, folding it down. Repeat until the whole strip is folded.

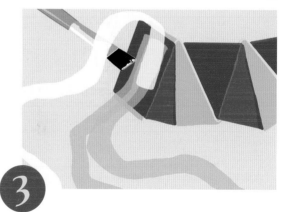

3 Cut strips of pink and white tissue paper and attach them to one end of the strip for a tail.

4 Draw a dragon's head onto thick white paper. Cut it out and paint it yellow or orange with a red mouth.

5 Paint a big eye surrounded by circles, two nostrils, and black lips. Add gold highlights to the face. Make two fringes from the yellow and green papers and stick to the neck. Add pink tissue to the forehead.

6 Use clear adhesive tape to attach a garden stake to the back of the dragon's head. Add another near the tail and your dragon puppet is ready to roar!

Christmas crackers

Make the family groan at Christmas. Put all your favorite terrible riddles in these homemade Christmas crackers.

You Will Need

- Crêpe paper
- Cardboard toilet-paper tubes
- Pinking shears
- Riddles on small pieces of paper
- Hardcandies in wrappers
- Cracker snaps
- Rubber band
- Sparkly pipe cleaners
- Shiny hologram tape. and glue
- Small gift bows: red and green

1 Use pinking shears to cut a piece of green crêpe paper three times as long as the toilet-paper tube and wide enough to go around it with a 1 inch overlap.

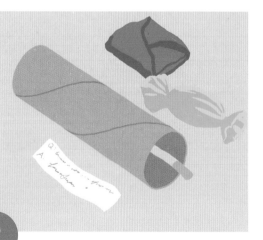

2 Put a wrapped candy, folded paper crown, joke and cracker snap in the toilet-paper tube.

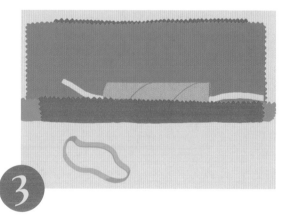

3 Cut red crêpe paper the same width but ¾ inch shorter than the green. Wrap both layers around the tube and hold them in place with a rubber band.

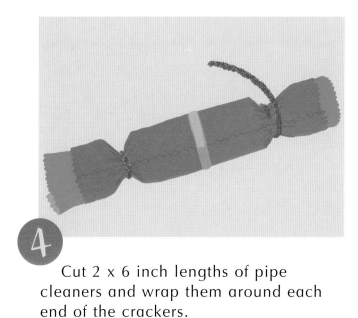

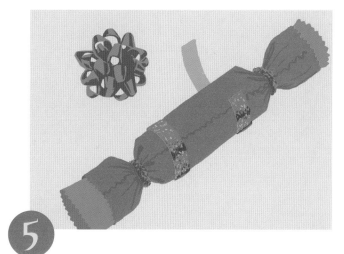

4 Cut 2 x 6 inch lengths of pipe cleaners and wrap them around each end of the crackers.

5 Cut 2 strips of hologram tape and glue them around the tube. Remove the rubber band and decorate the tube with a gift bow.

Try This!

Paper crowns

It's easy to make paper crowns. Cut a piece of tissue paper about 6 x 24 inches. Glue both ends together and fold it in half twice. Cut the paper to a point. Open it out and you have a crown!

179

Halloween bat card

When you've finished trick-or-treating, make a spooky bat silhouette card for a really horrid halloween gift!

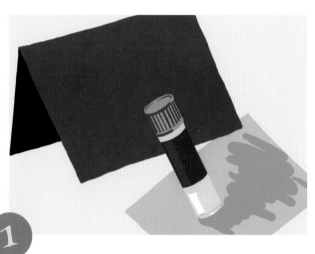

1 Fold the black card in half. Glue the orange paper to the front of the card, placing it centrally to leave a black border all around.

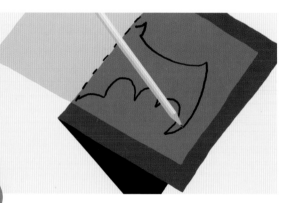

2 Trace the shape on p.221 onto tracing paper. Fold a sheet of black paper in half and put the tracing paper on top. Trace down the half-bat shape.

You Will Need

✦ 11 x 8 inch sheet of black cardboard
✦ Sheet of orange paper 4³/₄ x 7¹/₄ inches
✦ Tracing paper and pencil
✦ 8 x 5 inch sheet black paper
✦ Scissors
✦ Gluestick
✦ 2 round green sequins

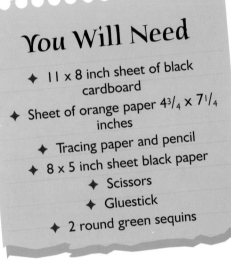

Top Tip

Trace marks can be difficult to see on the black paper. If you're good with scissors, cut out the bat instead. Line up the tracing paper so the edge of the bat is at the edge of the black paper. Grip both pieces of paper tightly and cut around the bat shape.

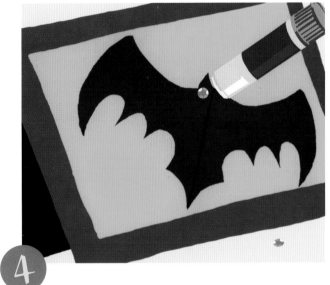

3 Cut out the half-bat, leaving the fold uncut. Open out the bat and apply glue all over it. Stick it down at an angle on the front of the card.

4 Stick on green sequins with a dab of glue to add menacing bat's eyes.

Chocolate nests

Make an Easter treat for the family with yummy chocolate nests. Don't forget to ask an adult to help.

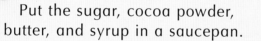
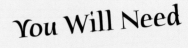

You Will Need

For 5 nests:
- ✦ Heaping ¹/₃ cup sugar
- ✦ ¹/₃ cup butter
- ✦ ¹/₂ cup cocoa powder
- ✦ 2 tbsp corn syrup
- ✦ 2 ¹/₂ ounces shredded wheat
- ✦ Aluminum foil
- ✦ Medium saucepan
- ✦ Metal spoon
- ✦ Mini chocolate eggs

1 Put the sugar, cocoa powder, butter, and syrup in a saucepan.

2 Place the pan on low heat and stir slowly until the mixture melts. Don't let it boil!

3 Let the mixture cool slightly. Crumble the shredded wheat and mix it in.

4 Make the aluminum foil into five bowl shapes. Put some mixture in and press in the middle to make nests. Put them in the fridge to cool and set.

5 When the nests are hard, remove the foil and fill the chocolate nests with mini eggs.

Hanukkah candlestick

Jewish people celebrate the Hanukkah festival by lighting special candles and exchanging gifts. This special candleholder is called a menorah.

1 Roll out the clay to ³/₄ inch. Put the template (see p.220) onto the clay and cut around it. On the flat end, using your toothpick, pierce nine small holes to mark the position of the candles.

You Will Need

- ✦ Tracing paper and pencil
- ✦ 18 ounces air-hardening clay
- ✦ Rolling pin
- ✦ Plastic knife
- ✦ Toothpick
- ✦ Ruler and old pen
- ✦ Gold paint and paintbrush
- ✦ 9 small candles

Make a mark on the pencil so you know how far down to push.

2 Push the end of the pencil about ¹/₂ inch into the holes. Do this for all except the middle hole which should only be ¹/₄ inch deep, so the candle will stand taller.

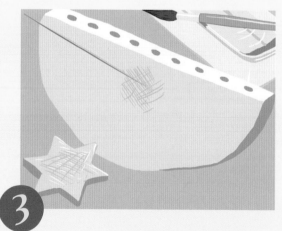

3 Roll out a small piece of clay and cut out a star using the template. Attach it to one side of the candlestick by wetting and scoring both pieces to help them stick.

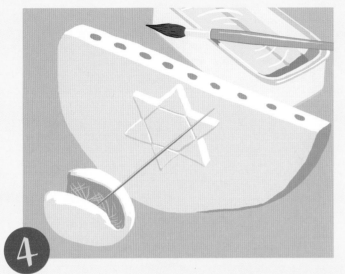

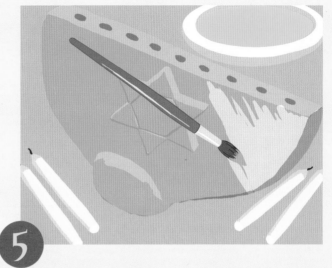

4 Roll a 2 inch ball of clay. Flatten the bottom and make a groove along the top. Stick it to the bottom of the candlestick. Make sure it stands firmly and leave it to dry.

5 Paint the candlestick gold all over and leave it to dry. Insert the nine candles into the candlestick holes and ask an adult to light them.

Snowmen card

Make these great cut-out Christmas cards for all your friends. They're 'snow' cool!

You Will Need

✦ 11 x 8 inch sheet white cardboard
✦ Pencil and ruler
✦ Scraps of black cardboard
✦ Felt-tipped pens
✦ Silver glitter
✦ White glue and brush

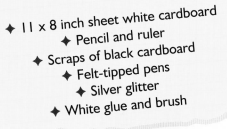

1 Mark the card along the long side, at 3³/₄ and 7³/₄ inches. Fold the card into three equal sections as shown.

Don't snip these edges!

2 Draw a snowman shape on the card. Cut out the snowman, leaving it joined at the sides.

Pudding card

Make a Christmas pudding card with brown-painted card. Draw around a small saucer, cut it out, and stick on some paper holly and berries.

Paint on a thin layer of glue and sprinkle on silver glitter for a sparkly finishing touch.

3 Open up the card. Cut three hats from the black cardboard and stick them on the snowmen's heads.

4 Use the felt-tipped pens to draw eyes, mouths, and buttons. Finish with orange carroty noses, brown canes, and scarves.

Advent calendar

Start your countdown to Christmas with this Advent calendar. Fill the boxes with your favorite candies and give yourself a daily treat while you wait!

1

Glue the green cardboard upright to the thick cardboard, leaving space at the top and bottom. Cut out a star from the gold cardboard and glue it at the top. Trim the edges of the red cardboard to make a pot shape and glue it at the bottom.

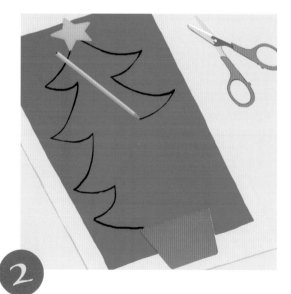

2

Draw a large Christmas tree shape on the green cardboard and cut the whole shape out.

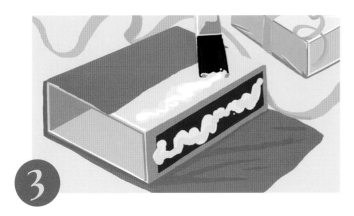

◀ Cover 12 matchboxes in red foil paper and 12 in silver. Tie a piece of gift ribbon around each matchbox and tie a double knot in it. Curl the ribbon by running it between your thumbnail and index finger.

3

4

Using the gold marker pen, number each of the small boxes from 1 to 23. Write "24" on the big matchbox. Put a wrapped candy or chocolate in each box, and put two in the 24 box.

5

Arrange boxes 1 to 23 randomly on the Christmas tree and put the 24 box in the middle. Glue all the boxes in place. Glue sequin stars onto the tree in the gaps between the boxes.

Mother's Day photo booklet

Your Mom will love to keep her favorite pictures of you in this elegant photo album.

You Will Need

◆ 2 pieces of cardboard 6 x 6 inches
◆ 2 sheets 11 x 8 inch purple paper
◆ Clear adhesive tape
◆ White glue
◆ 1 yard turquoise ribbon
◆ Sheet of turquoise paper 6 x 24 inches
◆ Pencil and ruler
◆ Blue corrugated card 4 x 4 inches
◆ Small square of purple felt
◆ Pnking shears
◆ Gems to decorate

1 Wrap each sheet of purple paper around a square of cardboard and fix in place with clear adhesive tape.

2 Cut the ribbon into four equal strips. Glue to the back of the purple cards, as shown above. Trim the end of each ribbon into a V shape.

3 Glue the end of the sheet of turquoise paper to the wrong side of one of the purple boards.

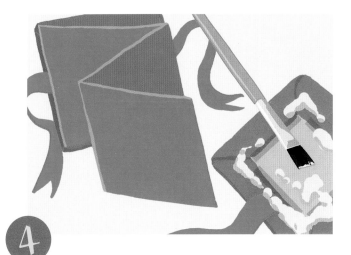

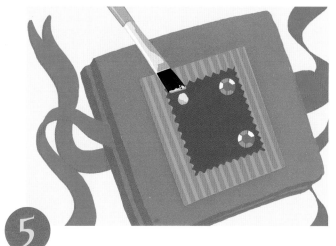

4 Fold the turquoise paper strip three times, accordian-style. Glue the last fold to the wrong side of the remaining purple board.

5 Decorate the front by sticking on some blue corrugated cardboard, then a smaller square of purple felt cut with pinking shears. Glue some gems to the felt as a finishing touch.

Cut triangles from purple felt to fix the corners of your photos in place.

Christmas stars

Are you in a hurry for Christmas?
Make some sparkly foil tree
decorations while you wait for
the big day.

You Will Need

✦ Thick card (i.e. laundry detergent)
✦ Tracing paper and pencil
✦ Scissors
✦ White glue
✦ Foil candy wrappers
✦ Sequin stars
✦ Hole punch
✦ Gold cord

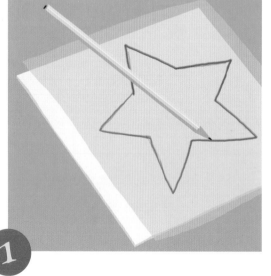

1 Trace the star from the template
on p.220. Put the tracing on the
card and draw over the lines to
transfer it to the card.

2 Use the scissors to cut out the
star design.

3

Tear the candy wrappers into small random pieces. Glue the pieces all over the star, overlapping them until the whole shape is covered. Leave to dry.

4

Glue sequin stars onto both sides of the foil-covered star. Leave to dry.

5

Use the hole punch to make a hole in one of the points of the star. Thread a length of gold cord through the hole and knot the ends together.

Try This!

Bells and trees

Make decorations in different shapes with a Christmas theme. You could try a green tree or a bell.

Halloween lantern

Halloween would not be complete without a glowing jack-o'-lantern. Put one in your window to greet trick-or-treaters.

You Will Need

- ✦ Medium-sized pumpkin
- ✦ Spoon or ice-cream scoop
- ✦ Felt-tipped pen
- ✦ Small knife
- ✦ Short, fat candle

1 Scoop out the insides of the pumpkin, using a spoon or an ice-cream scoop.

2 Use a felt-tipped pen to draw a scary face onto the pumpkin.

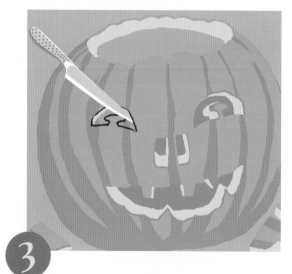

3 Now for the tricky part! Ask an adult to cut away the marked pattern, using a small knife.

4 Put a small candle inside the pumpkin and ask an adult to light it.

Try This!

Scary cat

You can make all kinds of faces on your pumpkin. This spooky witch's cat uses the stalk as a nose. Great idea!

Top Tip If your pumpkin dries out and looks withered, soak it in cold water for a few hours and it will be as good as new.

Nativity scene

This model looks beautiful and will help remind you of the wonderful story of the very first Christmas.

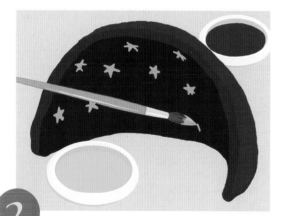

1 Make five thumb-shaped pieces of clay. These will be Mary, Joseph, and three shepherds. Make four sheep-shaped lumps. Make a small ball and press it in the middle to make a cradle. Flatten a tiny ball to make a baby that will fit in the cradle. Leave them to dry.

2 Roll out a fist-sized piece of clay and shape it into a cave. When it is hard and dry, paint the cave dark blue, with tiny gold stars all over the inside.

3 Paint Mary and Joseph, using a small brush. Give Mary a blue veil and Joseph a green robe. Wait for the paint to dry before adding the details on the faces.

Now paint the three shepherds with headdresses and bushy beards. Paint the sheep white, with black faces and feet.

4

5

Paint the cradle. Make the baby white, with black stripes to show that he is wrapped in a sheet. When it is dry, paint the baby's face and features.

Try This!

Three Kings
Add the Three Kings to your Christmas scene. Paint gold details on their clothes to make them look grand.

Golf paperweight

If your Dad plays golf he will like this Fathers' Day gift.

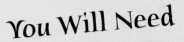

You Will Need

- ✦ Wooden doorknob
- ✦ Paints: white, green, red
- ✦ Paintbrush
- ✦ Air-drying clay
- ✦ Strong wood glue

1 Paint the doorknob white and the flat top green. Put little tufts of grass around the bottom.

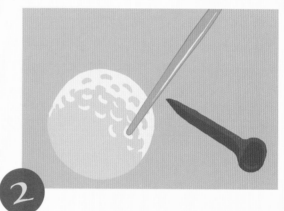

2 Roll a clay ball and make dimples with the end of the brush. Paint it white. Make a tee from the clay and paint it red.

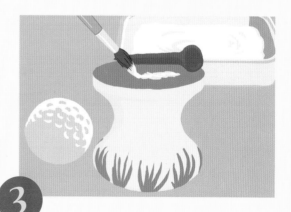

3 When the clay has hardened, glue the ball and the tee to the green surface and leave it to dry.

198

NATURECRAFT

Teasel mouse

A teasel is the dried head of a thistle. You can buy them in florists' or craft suppliers. They are really simple to turn one into cute little mice.

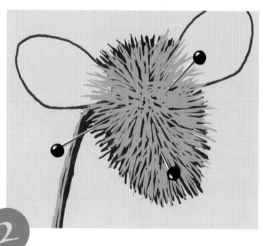

1 Draw two mouse-ear shapes. Color them pink with brown rims and cut them out.

You Will Need

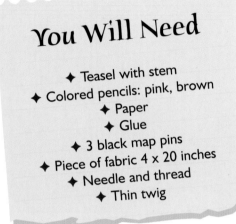

♦ Teasel with stem
♦ Colored pencils: pink, brown
♦ Paper
♦ Glue
♦ 3 black map pins
♦ Piece of fabric 4 x 20 inches
♦ Needle and thread
♦ Thin twig

2 Push the ears into the teasel head and glue them in. Push in three pins, for eyes and a nose. Gently bend the teasel down a little so that it points forward on its stalk.

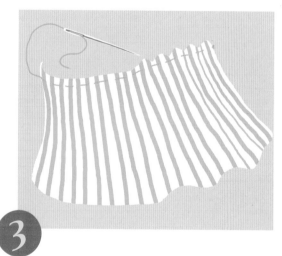

3 Make a dress by sewing a running stitch along one of the long edges of the fabric. Then pull the thread so that the fabric gathers up. Cut the thread and knot the end.

4 Put the teasel inside the dress. Cut a small slit in each side of the dress and thread through it a small twig to make arms.

Try This!

Pine cone owl

If you can't find a teasel, make Ollie the owl instead. Pine cones are easy to find in your local park. Give him leaf wings and feet, stick- on card eyes, and glasses made from some wire.

Shell jewelry box

Use seashells to make a luxurious jewelry box from a humble food container. Collect shells if you live near the beach, or buy a bag from a craft supplier.

You Will Need

+ Round food container with lid
+ 2 squares of red felt
+ Pencil
+ Scissors
+ White glue and brush
+ Blue acrylic paint and brush
+ Assorted seashells

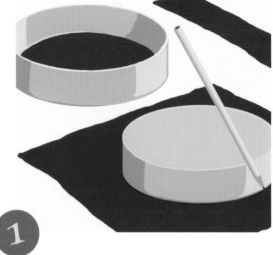

1 Draw around the lid of the box onto the red felt. Cut it out, and stick it inside the lid. Repeat, and stick onto the base of the box.

2 Measure the depth of the box and cut a long strip of felt the same width. Glue it around the inside of the box, trimming the ends to make it fit neatly.

3 Paint the sides, the base, and the outside of the lid with acrylic paint.

Mini shell boxes

Tiny boxes can be decorated with a single shell. Use them as gift boxes for earrings and brooches you made for yourself.

4 Arrange the shells on the box lid and glue them on.

Twig furniture

Collect twigs from the backyard or your local park. Use them to make fun furniture, perhaps for a doll's house.

You Will Need

+ About 30 thin twigs
+ Scissors
+ Wood glue
+ Brush

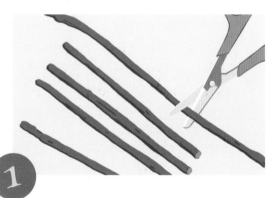

1 To make a chair, cut 15 thin sticks about $1\frac{1}{2}$ inches long.

2 Put nine sticks side by side and glue two sticks at either end to hold them together.

3 Cut two $4\frac{3}{4}$ inch sticks for the back of the chair. Glue the seat halfway up the sticks. Glue two front legs, $2\frac{1}{4}$ inches long, to the front of the seat.

4 Glue four sticks around the bottom of the chair, and one at the top. Glue two sticks diagonally to the back to make a cross.

5 To make a table, glue eight sticks with a shorter stick at either end.

6 Glue four legs to the table top, then make the table sturdy by gluing two long and two short twigs to the legs, and two long twigs crosswise under the table.

Top Tip You can make little chair cushions by cutting out a piece of fabric twice as long as the chair seat. Glue three sides, stuff it with cotton batting and glue the two edges together.

Cactus garden

You don't need to be an expert to grow a cactus garden. A sunny windowsill and some water once a week are all these prickly customers need.

You Will Need

◆ 5 small assorted cacti
◆ Bowl large enough for all 5 cacti
◆ Cactus soil mix
◆ Wad of paper towels
◆ Old spoon
◆ Colored gravel

To move the cactus without pricking yourself on the spines, wrap a thick wad of paper towel round it.

1 Put a thin layer of gravel in the bottom of the bowl. Add a layer of compost to within $3/4$ inch of the top of the bowl. Use your finger to make a hole in the soil mix toward the back of the bowl with your hands.

2 Choose the tallest cactus and remove it from its pot. Put it in the hole you have made and use your fingers to push down the soil mix firmly all around it.

Top Tip If you don't have colored gravel, make a desert garden instead by spreading sand on top of the soil mix.

3 Make another hole in the soil mix and plant the next tallest cactus in the same way as before.

4 Continue planting. Use an old spoon to press down the soil mix firmly around the base of each cactus.

5 Using the spoon, arrange the gravel around the base of each cactus until the soil mix is covered.

Pebble porcupine family

The best pebbles for painting are the smooth type you can find on the beach. Keep an eye out for suitable ones on your next trip to the seaside.

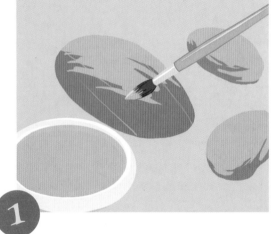

You Will Need

+ 1 large and 2 small smooth stones
+ Acrylic paints: gray, black, and white
+ Paintbrushes: medium and small
+ Clear varnish

1 Wash and dry the stones. Paint them gray all over and leave them to dry. Paint an extra coat if you need to.

2 Use the fine paintbrush to paint black bristles all over the tops of the pebbles.

3

Paint on a black nose and add nostrils by painting white circles with black dots in the middle. For eyes, make two black circles, smaller white circles inside, and black dots in the middle. Now paint the baby porcupines in the same way.

4

If the porcupines are going to live on the doorstep or in the backyard, give them all a coat of clear varnish.

Try This!

Gorgeous goldfish

You can make all kinds of pebble creatures. Look at the shape of the pebble and see what it reminds you of. This one has been turned into a scaly goldfish.

Garden on a plate

Making a miniature garden will keep you busy on a rainy day. Collect tiny cuttings of shrubs and flowers from the garden and get painting!

You Will Need

- Old dinner plate
- Soil mix
- Moss, grass, and small flowers, such as daisies
- Cuttings from shrubs
- Fir tree twig
- Kitchen foil
- Jam jar lid
- 2 twigs and string
- Paper and colored pencils
- Scissors

1 Put a ¼ inch layer of soil mix on the plate. Press moss into about three-quaters of the area.

2 Put small pebbles around the plate edge and make a path of pebbles in the soil, as shown.

3 Push a fir twig into the soil to make a miniature tree. Push the flowers, shrubs, and grass into the soil.

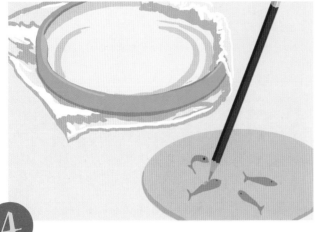

4 Mold kitchen foil around a jam jar lid to make a pond. Cut out a circle to fit in the bottom of the pond. Color it blue, and draw some goldfish onto it. Put some more blades of grass around the pond to look like reeds.

5 Draw some clothes on a piece of white paper, giving them tags so you can hang them on a washing line. Color them and cut them out.

Top Tip Spray your garden with water to keep it fresh. Replace the flowers when they begin to wilt.

6 Make a washing line from twigs and string. Hide two small pieces of plasticine in the moss and push the twigs into them. Glue the clothes to the line.

Pressed-flower card

Pressed flowers can be used to make beautiful greeting cards. Don't forget to check with an adult before you pick their favorite flowers!

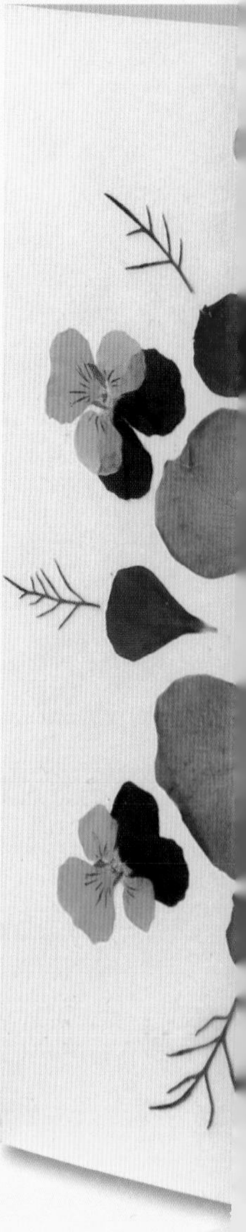

You Will Need

- Flowers and leaves
- Heavy books
- Paper towels
- White glue mixed with equal amount of water
- Cream cardboard 16 x 18 inches
- Scissors and ruler

◀ Pick some flower petals and leaves. Arrange them on paper towels, then put another piece of paper towel on top. Place them inside a book.

212

1

2 Place a pile of heavy books on top of the book with the flower, petals, and leaves inside. Leave them for at least two weeks.

3 Fold the cream cardboard in half and make a sharp crease with the outside of the scissors and a ruler.

4 Remove the pressed petals and leaves from the book. Arrange them on the front of the card and glue them into position.

213

Bottle garden

If you'd like a garden but you don't like the idea of all that weeding and mowing the lawn, this bottle garden is for you. Just remember to water it once a week and your plants will be happy.

You Will Need

✦ Large glass jar with lid
✦ Clear adhesive tape
✦ Old spoon
✦ Cotton ball
✦ 2 wooden skewers
✦ Colored gravel
✦ Soil mix
✦ Small plants

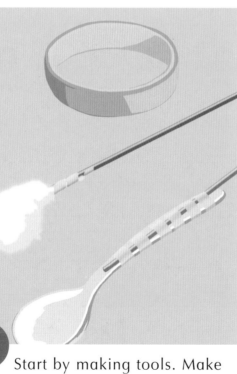

1 Start by making tools. Make a digger by taping a spoon to a wooden skewer, using lots of adhesive tape. Make a cleaning tool by taping a cotton ball to the other stick.

2 Spoon about 1½ inches of colored gravel into the bottom of the jar.

3 Now add about 3 inches of moist soil mix and press it down with your hands.

4 Use the spoon and your hands to make a hole and put a small plant in it. Press down firmly around the base, then put in two or three more plants.

5 Dip the cotton ball in water and squeeze it out. Use your cleaning tool to wipe away any smears of soil mix from the sides of the jar.

Make your bottle garden more interesting with a tropical bird on a stick. Look for these in garden centers.

215

Leaf puppet

Here's a bright idea for a fall day. Why not collect some interesting leaves and make a puppet, complete with leafy outfit?

1 Draw a face and neck about 1½ inches long. Color in the face and give her eyes, nose, and a mouth but no hair! Cut the shape out.

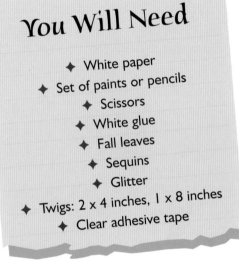

3 Glue small pointed leaves around the face to make hair. Glue leaves onto the dress, starting with large leaves at the bottom, and using smaller ones nearer the waist.

2 Draw, color in, and cut out a dress shape, about 6 inches long. Glue the head to the dress.

◄ Glue sequins to the neck, sleeves, and waist of the dress, then dot some over the leaves. Brush a little glue on the leaf edges, then sprinkle glitter over them. Leave to dry.

4

5

Turn the figure over and stick a small twig to each sleeve with tape. Tape a long twig up the length of the puppet, leaving about 4 inches at the bottom.

Sand butterfly

Did you know you can paint with sand? It sounds crazy, but you can make amazing textured pictures. Buy sets of colored sand from craft suppliers.

1 Fold the white paper in half and draw half a butterfly's body and a wing. Cut it out. Unfold the shape and put it on the sheet of blue cardboard at an angle.

You Will Need

✦ 11 x 8 inch sheet of blue card
✦ 11 x 8 inch sheet of white paper and pencil
✦ Scissors
✦ Black felt-tipped pen
✦ 16 ½ x 11 ¾ inch sheet scrap paper
✦ White glue and stiff brush
✦ Coloured sand: red, orange, yellow ocher, blue, green
✦ Teaspoon

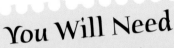

2 Use the black felt-tipped pen to draw around the outline, then put on markings, matching the pattern on each wing.

3 Place the scrap paper under the card. Paste a thin layer of white glue over the butterfly's body and head only.

4 Pour some yellow-ocher sand into the spoon and sprinkle over the glued area. Lift the picture with both hands and gently tap the spare sand onto the scrap paper. Pour the sand carefully back into its container.

5 Continue gluing and sprinkling, working on a small area at a time so the glue does not dry out before you add the sand.

Try This!

Dragonfly

This shimmering dragonfly is made in the same way as the butterfly. The white background makes the colorful sand really stand out.

Top templates

Draw around these shapes with a pencil onto tracing paper, then turn the tracing paper over lay on plain paper and scribble over the lines.

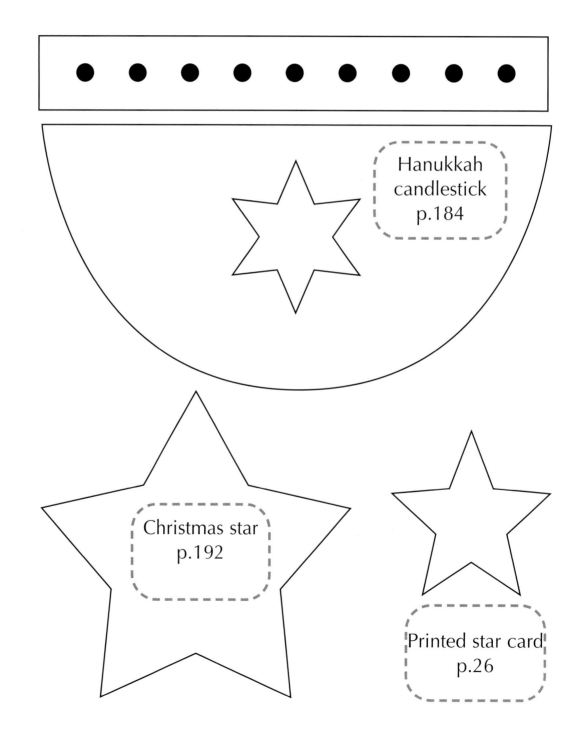

Hanukkah candlestick p.184

Christmas star p.192

Printed star card p.26

Halloween bat
card
p.180

Dinosaur
mail holder
p.16

221

Royal crown
p.164

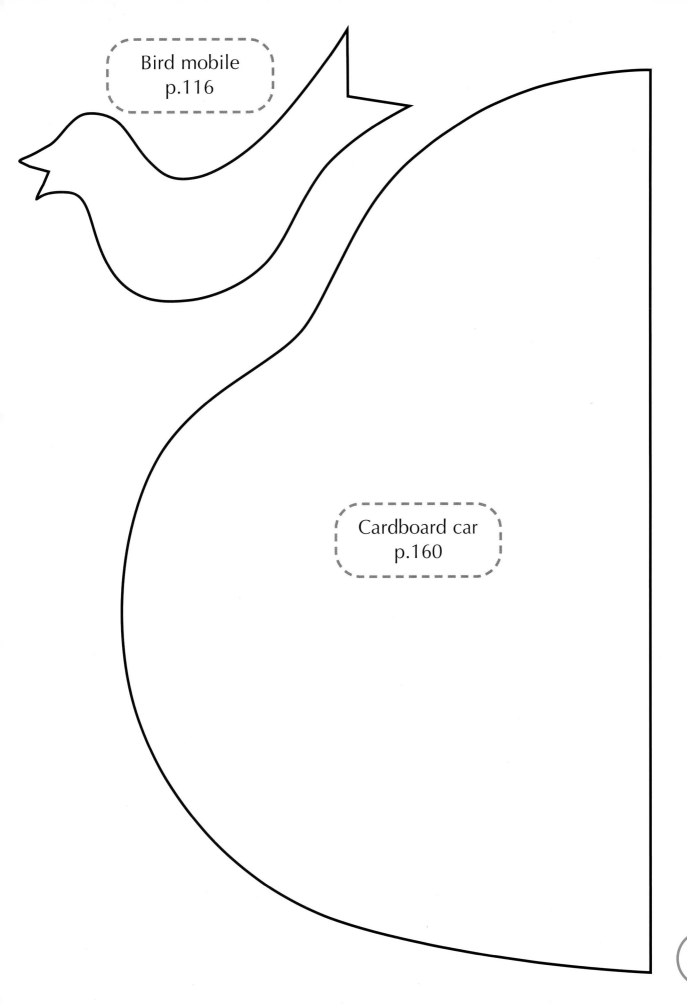

Bird mobile
p.116

Cardboard car
p.160

Index

Credits

Project creators: Anita Ruddell
                 Melanie Williams
Illustrator: Gary Walton

Photographer: John Englefield
Project editor: Rona Skene
Produced by DropCap Ltd